THE COMMON LAW CONSTITUTION

For the 2013 Hamlyn Lectures, Sir Jon Laws explored the constitutional balance between law and government in the United Kingdom. He argues that the unifying principle on the constitution is the common law and that its distinctive method has endowed the British State with profoundly beneficial effects, before examining two contemporary threats to the constitutional balance: extremism and the effect of Europe-made laws on the domestic English system.

SIR JOHN LAWS has served in the Court of Appeal and Privy Council since 1999. He has been responsible for a large number of important cases, including Thoburn v. Sunderland City Council which confronted the twin powers of Westminster and Brussels. Sir John is also a constitutional jurist of note, having written several extra-judicial contributions that underline the importance of the rule of law and the courts in a democracy so that sovereignty is founded in the constitution, not just parliament.

THE COMMON LAW CONSTITUTION

SIR JOHN LAWS

CAMBRIDGE
UNIVERSITY PRESS

CAMBRIDGE
UNIVERSITY PRESS

University Printing House, Cambridge CB2 8BS, United Kingdom

Cambridge University Press is part of the University of Cambridge.

It furthers the University's mission by disseminating knowledge in the pursuit of education, learning and research at the highest international levels of excellence.

www.cambridge.org
Information on this title: www.cambridge.org/9781107077720

First published 2014

A catalogue record for this publication is available from the British Library

Library of Congress Cataloguing in Publication data
Laws, John, 1945– author.
The common law constitution / John Laws.
pages cm – (The Hamlyn lectures)
Includes bibliographical references and index.
ISBN 978-1-107-07772-0 (Hardback)
1. Common law – Great Britain. 2. Constitutional law – Great Britain. 3. Common law – Philosophy. I. Title.
KD671.L395 2014
342.42–dc23
2014013706

ISBN 978-1-107-07772-0 Hardback
ISBN 978-1-107-43465-3 Paperback

CONTENTS

The Hamlyn Trust *page* vi

The Hamlyn Lectures ix

Preface and acknowledgements xiii

The Common Law Constitution, *Hamlyn Lectures 2013* 1

Lecture I The Common Law and State Power 3

Lecture II The Common Law and Extremism 31

Lecture III The Common Law and Europe 57

Index 87

THE HAMLYN TRUST

The Hamlyn Trust owes its existence today to the will of the late Miss Emma Warburton Hamlyn of Torquay, who died in 1941 at the age of eighty. She came of an old and well-known Devon family. Her father, William Bussell Hamlyn, practised in Torquay as a solicitor and Justice of the Peace for many years, and it seems likely that Miss Hamlyn founded the trust in his memory. Emma Hamlyn was a woman of strong character, intelligent and cultured, well-versed in literature, music and art, and a lover of her country. She travelled extensively in Europe and Egypt, and apparently took considerable interest in the law and ethnology of the countries and cultures that she visited. An account of Miss Hamlyn by Prof. Chantal Stebbings of the University of Exeter may be found, under the title 'The Hamlyn Legacy', in volume 42 of the published Lectures.

Miss Hamlyn bequeathed the residue of her estate on trust in terms which it seems were her own. The wording was thought to be vague, and the will was taken to the Chancery Division of the High Court, which in November 1948 approved a Scheme for the administration of the trust. Paragraph 3 of the Scheme, which follows Miss Hamlyn's own wording, is as follows:

> The object of the charity is the furtherance by lectures or otherwise among the Common People of the United

> Kingdom of Great Britain and Northern Ireland of the knowledge of the Comparative Jurisprudence and Ethnology of the Chief European countries including the United Kingdom, and the circumstances of the growth of such jurisprudence to the Intent that the Common People of the United Kingdom may realise the privileges which in law and custom they enjoy in comparison with other European Peoples and realising and appreciating such privileges may recognise the responsibilities and obligations attaching to them.

The Trustees are to include the Vice-Chancellor of the University of Exeter, representatives of the Universities of London, Leeds, Glasgow, Belfast and Wales and persons co-opted. At present there are eight Trustees:

From the outset it was decided that the objects of the Trust could be best achieved by means of an annual course of public lectures of outstanding interest and quality by eminent lecturers, and by their subsequent publication and distribution to a wider audience. The first of the Lectures were delivered by the Rt Hon. Lord Justice Denning (as he then was) in 1949. Since then there has been an unbroken series of annual Lectures published until 2005 by Sweet & Maxwell, and from 2006 by Cambridge University Press. A complete list of the Lectures may be found on pp. ix to xii. In 2005 the Trustees decided to supplement the Lectures with an annual Hamlyn Seminar, normally held at the Institute of Advanced Legal Studies in the University of London, to mark the publication of the Lectures in printed book form. The Trustees have also, from time to time, provided financial support for a variety of projects which, in various ways, have disseminated knowledge or have promoted to a wider public understanding of the law.

This, the 65th series of Lectures, was delivered by Sir John Laws at Northumbria University, Exeter College, Oxford and Inner Temple Hall, London. The Board of Trustees would like to record its appreciation to Sir John Laws and also the three venues which generously hosted these Lectures.

AVROM SHERR
Chairman of the Trustees

1949 'Freedom under the Law' by Rt Hon. Lord Denning
1950 'The Inheritance of the Common Law' by Richard O'Sullivan
1951 'The Rational Strength of English Law' by Prof. F. H. Lawson
1952 'English Law and the Moral Law' by Prof. A. L. Goodhart
1953 'The Queen's Peace' by Sir Carleton Kemp Allen
1954 'Executive Discretion and Judicial Control' by Prof. C. J. Hamson
1955 'The Proof of Guilt' by Prof. Glanville Williams
1956 'Trial by Jury' by Rt Hon. Lord Devlin
1957 'Protection from Power under English Law' by Rt Hon. Lord MacDermott
1958 'The Sanctity of Contracts in English Law' by Prof. Sir David Hughes Parry
1959 'Judge and Jurist in the Reign of Victoria' by C. H. S. Fifoot
1960 'The Common Law in India' by M. C. Setalvad
1961 'British Justice: The Scottish Contribution' by Prof. Sir Thomas Smith
1962 'Lawyer and Litigant in England' by Rt Hon. Sir Robert Megarry
1963 'Crime and the Criminal Law' by Baroness Wootton of Abinger
1964 'Law and Lawyers in the United States' by Dean Erwin N. Griswold

1965 'New Law for a New World?' by Rt Hon. Lord Tangley

1966 'Other People's Law' by Rt Hon. Lord Kilbrandon

1967 'The Contribution of English Law to South African Law, and the Rule of Law in South Africa' by Hon. O. D. Schreiner

1968 'Justice in the Welfare State' by Prof. H. Street

1969 'The British Tradition in Canadian Law' by Hon. Bora Laskin

1970 'The English Judge' by Henry Cecil

1971 'Punishment, Prison and the Public' by Prof. Sir Rupert Cross

1972 'Labour and the Law' by Prof. Sir Otto Kahn-Freund

1973 'Maladministration and its Remedies' by Sir Kenneth Wheare

1974 'English Law: The New Dimension' by Rt Hon. Lord Scarman

1975 'The Land and the Development; or, The Turmoil and the Torment' by Sir Desmond Heap

1976 'The National Insurance Commissioners' by Sir Robert Micklethwait

1977 'The European Communities and the Rule of Law' by Lord Mackenzie Stuart

1978 'Liberty, Law and Justice' by Prof. Sir Norman Anderson

1979 'Social History and Law Reform' by Prof. Lord McGregor of Durris

1980 'Constitutional Fundamentals' by Prof. Sir William Wade

1981 'Intolerable Inquisition? Reflections on the Law of Tax' by Hubert Monroe

1982 'The Quest for Security: Employees, Tenants, Wives' by Prof. Tony Honoré

1983 'Hamlyn Revisited: The British Legal System Today' by Lord Hailsham of St Marylebone
1984 'The Development of Consumer Law and Policy: Bold Spirits and Timorous Souls' by Sir Gordon Borrie
1985 'Law and Order' by Prof. Ralf Dahrendorf
1986 'The Fabric of English Civil Justice' by Sir Jack Jacob
1987 'Pragmatism and Theory in English Law' by Prof. P. S. Atiyah
1988 'Justification and Excuse in the Criminal Law' by Prof. J. C. Smith
1989 'Protection of the Public: A New Challenge' by Rt Hon. Lord Justice Woolf
1990 'The United Kingdom and Human Rights' by Dr Claire Palley
1991 'Introducing a European Legal Order' by Gordon Slynn
1992 'Speech and Respect' by Prof. Richard Abel
1993 'The Administration of Justice' by Lord Mackay of Clashfern
1994 'Blackstone's Tower: The English Law School' by Prof. William Twining
1995 'From the Test Tube to the Coffin: Choice and Regulation in Private Life' by Hon. Mrs Justice Hale
1996 'Turning Points of the Common Law' by Rt Hon. Lord Cooke of Thorndon
1997 'Commercial Law in the Next Millennium' by Prof. Roy Goode
1998 'Freedom, Law and Justice' by Rt Hon. Lord Justice Sedley
1999 'The State of Justice' by Prof. Michael Zander QC
2000 'Does the United Kingdom Still have a Constitution?' by Prof. Anthony King

2001	'Human Rights, Serious Crime and Criminal Procedure' by Prof. Andrew Ashworth QC
2002	'Legal Conundrums in Our Brave New World' by Baroness Kennedy of the Shaws
2003	'Judicial Activism' by Hon. Justice Michael Kirby AC, CMG
2004	'Rights at Work: Global, European and British Perspectives' by Sir Bob Hepple QC, FBA
2005	'Can Human Rights Survive?' by Prof. Conor Gearty
2006	'The Sovereignty of Law: The European Way' by Sir Francis Jacobs KCMG, QC
2007	'The Prisoners' Dilemma' by Prof. Nicola Lacey
2008	'Judging Civil Justice' by Dame Hazel Genn
2009	'Widening Horizons: The Influence of Comparative Law and International Law on Domestic Law' by Lord Bingham
2010	'Lawyers and the Public Good: Democracy in Action?' by Alan Paterson
2011	'The Rule of Law and the Measure of Property' by Jeremy Waldron
2012	'Aspects of Law Reform: An Insider's Perspective' by Jack Straw

PREFACE AND ACKNOWLEDGEMENTS

The law is not a science, for its purpose is not to find out natural facts. It is an art as architecture is an art: its function is practical, but it is enhanced by such qualities as elegance, economy and clarity. The law has two practical purposes: first, to require, forbid or penalise forms of conduct between citizen and citizen, and citizen and state; secondly, to provide formal rules for classes of human activity whose fulfilment would otherwise be confused, uncertain or ineffective. Laws in the former category include every provision for a remedy, criminal and civil; those in the latter include all prescribed formalities and rules of procedure. All of the laws ought to be elegant, economical and clear; but it is a harder thing for the judge-made common law, which unlike statute is never a single work, but created over time.

In these Lectures I have been concerned with the first of these two purposes as it applies in the law of the constitution. In Lecture I, I describe the common law's fourfold method – evolution, experiment, history and distillation; its process of continuous self-correction, at once allowed and restrained by these four methods; and the benign implications which all this has for the means of our governance.

Lecture II confronts the challenges which our law faces in the shadow of extremism, and shows how the common law is enriched by insights from an older past: by Euthyphro's dilemma in the Platonic dialogue, rewritten thus – are laws or policies willed by the state because they are good, or are they good because they are willed by the state? – and by the petition of Aurelius Symmachus in AD 382: 'We look on the same stars, the heaven is common to us all, the same world surrounds us. What matters it by what arts each of us seeks for truth? We cannot arrive by one and the same path at so great a secret'.

In Lecture III I consider the challenges offered to the common law constitution by the influx of law from Europe: from Luxembourg and from Strasbourg. The common law is enriched by our legal importations from Europe: proportionality, legitimate expectation, and others; but there are fears of a loss of autonomy – to a considerable extent, in the human rights field, by our own courts' reluctance over the last few years to forge a domestic human rights jurisprudence.

The Lectures are almost as I delivered them; I have had one or two afterthoughts, and added one or two further references. I have throughout had very much in mind the purpose of the Hamlyn Trust, expressed in Miss Hamlyn's own words:

> to the Intent that the Common People of the United Kingdom may realise the privileges which in law and custom they enjoy in comparison with other European Peoples and realising and appreciating such privileges may recognise the responsibilities and obligations attaching to them.

The common law is the unifying principle of our constitution under the Crown; and I am sure it is the distinction of the common law that Miss Hamlyn had in mind. If I may anticipate Lecture I:

> The common law is not *dirigiste*. Its principles are constantly renewed by the force of fresh examples. It is not by chance that our constitution is uncodified; it is because, being conditioned over the centuries by the changing common law, it is not and cannot be the creature of a single moment. The elusive strength of the common law of England is that it reflects and moderates the temper of the people as age succeeds age. It is especially fit for a democratic state, for it builds on the experience of ordinary struggles. It stands for no grand theory of anything, but it is endlessly creative. Although it is much older, it enshrines a cardinal principle of the Enlightenment: that people should think for themselves.

By force of these characteristics, the law's purpose to require, forbid or penalise forms of conduct between citizen and citizen, and citizen and state, is fulfilled by an enriching combination of principle and flexibility: of old roots and new growth. Those privileged to practise in the common law may therefore be involved not only in applying it, but in creating it; and in doing so they will surely always have in mind the art of the law: its enhancement by elegance, economy and clarity.

I have tried to convey something of the common law's dynamic. In over forty years in its service I have learnt that it is always and never the same; and that it knows the difference between balance and compromise, and between dogma and principle.

I owe thanks to more friends and colleagues, old and new, than I can name. To my pupil master of forty-three years ago, Bill Macpherson (Sir William Macpherson of Cluny) from whom I learnt so much, not least the good sense of the common law; to Professor Avrom Sherr, whose warmth and encouragement has sped these Lectures on their way; to my fellow judges, for their intellectual generosity and good fellowship; and to the members of the three institutions where I was privileged to give the lectures – Northumbria University, Exeter College, Oxford and the Inner Temple, London. I hope they will all think the enterprise has been worthwhile. And last but first, to my dear wife Sophie, *sine qua nihil.*

The Common Law Constitution,
Hamlyn Lectures 2013

Sir John Laws

LECTURE I

The Common Law and State Power

Under the Crown, the unifying principle of our constitution is the common law. The common law's distinctive method has endowed the British state with profoundly beneficial effects.

In this Lecture I will explain why this is so. I will say that by force of the common law, efficacy is allowed but oppression is forbidden to the power of the state; and this is achieved by a benign *continuum* of developing law. I will tell what is a constitution's unifying principle, and what is the distinctive method of our constitution's unifying principle, the common law. I will give two instances of changes wrought without revolution by the common law's processes; the first concerns the sovereignty of Parliament, the second the judicial review jurisdiction. Then I will explain how Parliament's legislation only has effect through the methods of the common law. The common law is the interpreter of our statutes, and is the crucible which gives them life. The process of interpretation is intensely coloured by the common law's insights of substantive principle: reason, fairness and the presumption of liberty. So is the judicial review of executive action. The result is that statute law and government policy are alike delivered to the people through the prism of such principles. This is the gift of the common law, the unifying principle of our constitution. It is the means by which legislature and government are allowed efficacy but forbidden oppression.

This process both requires and produces a delicate constitutional balance between law and government. This Lecture is about the nature of this balance and its benign effects. In this context I will explain how the sovereignty of Parliament ought now to be understood. But there are two contemporary threats to the constitutional balance. The first is that present-day fears, real and imagined, of the grip of extremism exert an unwanted, perhaps dangerous, pressure on the moderate liberality of the common law. I will explain and confront this in Lecture II, 'The Common Law and Extremism'. The second is that the actual or perceived effects of law made in Europe upon our domestic system may undermine virtues of the common law: its catholicity and its restraint. I will explain and confront this in Lecture III, 'The Common Law and Europe'.

What is a Constitution's 'Unifying Principle'?

The term 'constitution' means, at least, that set of laws which in a sovereign state establish the relationship between the ruler and the ruled. Law in one form or another is therefore a defining element of every constitution, save in a territory where the people are ruled by the brute commands of whoever is the strongest leader from time to time; but we would deny the term 'constitution' to so coarse a state of affairs. In a constitutional state the sovereign is always a body whose designation, as R. T. E. Latham put it, 'must include the statement of rules for the ascertainment of his will, and those rules, since their observance is a condition of the validity of his legislation, are rules of law logically prior to him'.[1] The laws of the constitution will also contain definitions of the powers and duties of the sovereign, and the exercise of these powers will mark the reach of individual freedom in the state.

Such laws make the constitution. This is true of every constitution, written or unwritten, exotic or familiar, common law or civilian; for laws of this kind are what a constitution means. But written constitutions of the modern age typically contain much else besides. These are usually prescriptions, often framed in terms of rights, for the proper exercise of the sovereign's powers and duties. Such prescriptions are not a necessary condition of a constitution properly so called; but where they are found, they take their place among the constitution's provisions.

Law, then, is the unifying principle of every constitution; every constitution is made with a set of laws which (a) define the ruler and in doing so establish the relationship between the ruler and the ruled; and (b) contain definitions of the powers and duties of the sovereign. A constitution will also generally include (c) principles for the proper exercise of the sovereign's powers and duties. In the British state (a), (b) and (c) are given by an amalgam of the common law and statute, without a sovereign text. Statute has provided important pillars in the edifice, such as the Act of Union 1707, the legislation which confers the franchise, and the devolution legislation: all these go to (a) – they define the ruler. The Magna Carta of 1215, the Bill of Rights of 1689 and the

[1] R. T. E. Latham, *The Law and the Commonwealth* (Oxford University Press, 1949), p. 523 note 4.

European Communities Act 1972 go to (b) – they define, in part, the sovereign's powers and duties. It is important to note that the European Communities Act goes to (b) rather than (a), for it means that at law there has been no transfer of state sovereignty from Westminster to Brussels (but this is to trespass into Lecture III). The Human Rights Act 1998 goes to (c) (principles for the proper exercise of the sovereign's powers and duties).

Now, every one of these statutes, and every other statute, is mediated to the people by the common law. An Act of Parliament is words on a page. Only the common law gives it life. It is a commonplace to say that the judges interpret legislation, and so they do. But as I shall explain more fully, this is the opposite of an austere linguistic exercise. The construction of statutes, just as surely as the development of common law principles not touched by legislation, is the product of the common law's reason matured over time. The force of our constitution's provisions – (a), (b) and (c) above – is therefore delivered by the common law and its distinctive method. The unifying principle of our constitution is the common law. So I turn to my second topic: what is the common law's distinctive method?

The Common Law's Distinctive Method

I have said before that the method of the common law is fourfold: evolution, experiment, history and distillation.[2]

[2] I developed this description of the common law's method in the ICLR Annual Lecture, which I was privileged to give on 1 March 2012 under the title 'Our Lady of the Common Law'.

I referred earlier to the common law's insights: reason, fairness and the presumption of liberty. But they are enriched and matured through the law's fourfold method. Evolution – rules of law honed through the doctrine of precedent; experiment – working hypotheses discarded if they are not robust; history – the power of continuity; distillation – the modification and adjustment of the law to meet new conditions. Plainly these methods run into each other. They are the matrix of the common law's genius, which is the refinement of principle over time. Generally, they involve what may be described as reasoning from the bottom up, not the top down. The common law is not *dirigiste*. Its principles are constantly renewed by the force of fresh examples. It is not by chance that our constitution is uncodified; it is because, being conditioned over the centuries by the changing common law, it is not and cannot be the creature of a single moment. The elusive strength of the common law of England is that it reflects and moderates the temper of the people as age succeeds age. It is especially fit for a democratic state, for it builds on the experience of ordinary struggles. It stands for no grand theory of anything, but it is endlessly creative. Although it is much older, it enshrines a cardinal principle of the Enlightenment: that people should think for themselves.

To give these generalities sharper focus, I will say a little more about the common law's fourfold method: evolution, experiment, history and distillation.

(1) Evolution. By this I mean that rules of law are honed through the doctrine of precedent. It is to be noted that the law of *stare decisis* prescribes that although the Court of

Appeal binds itself, neither the Supreme Court nor the High Court does so. Thus precedent strikes a balance between certainty and adaptability. But there is a more subtle effect. It is that every principle has a tried and tested pedigree. It is refined out of what has gone before. It is never constructed from untried materials. Accordingly, every principle has deep foundations.

(2) Experiment. This is closely related to the evolutionary process which inheres in the doctrine of precedent. It was the American writer, Munroe Smith, who said in 1909 that '[t]he rules and principles of case law have never been treated as final truths, but as working hypotheses, continually retested in those great laboratories of the law, the courts of justice'.[3] If the analogy is not pressed too far, this is not unlike Prof. Sir Karl Popper's theory of scientific discovery first published in 1934:[4] science proceeds by postulating hypotheses which are only good so long as they are not disproved. So also a common law principle works until new experience shows it must be changed or abandoned.

(3) History. The common law's respect for our history is an important driver of a principal virtue of the constitution: the power of continuity. In this respect the law's wisdom is the wisdom of Edmund Burke's vision of society as a

[3] Quoted by Benjamin Cardozo in the first of his lectures on *The Nature of the Judicial Process* (Yale University Press, 1921). Munroe Smith (d. 1926) was a distinguished legal academic at Columbia University. He was managing editor of *Political Science Quarterly* for many years.

[4] *The Logic of Scientific Discovery* (1934).

contract between the living, the dead and those who are not yet born.[5]

(4) Distillation. This is the modification and adjustment of old law so that it becomes new. Authority exposes and then mends the law's weaknesses. A new case articulates the law's present state. But in doing so, it also clears its future path.

I have said that these four methods – evolution, experiment, history and distillation – run into each other. It might be more accurate to say that they are four aspects or dimensions of a single process. It is the process of continuous self-correction, which is at once allowed and restrained by the law's four methods. Its fruit is the common law's genius, the refinement of principle over time. The common law reflects and moderates the temper of the people as age succeeds age. It stands for no grand theory of anything, but it is endlessly creative. It is the crucible of the moderate and orderly development of state power.

The common law has had no Justinian, whose summations of the Roman law in the sixth century after Christ have proved the foundation of civilian codes of law in Europe to the present day. Gibbon has this to say:[6]

> When Justinian ascended the throne, the reformation of the Roman jurisprudence was an arduous but indispensable task ... Books could not easily be found; and the judges, poor in the midst of riches, were reduced to the exercise of their illiterate discretion.

5 Burke, *Reflections on the Revolution in France*.

6 Gibbon, *Decline and Fall of the Roman Empire*, vol. V, ch. 44.

And so, as Gibbon tells us, the Emperor directed Tribonian 'and nine learned associates to revise the ordinances of his predecessors'. Gibbon continues:[7]

> As soon as the emperor had approved their labours, he ratified, by his legislative power, the speculations of these private citizens: their commentaries on the twelve tables, the perpetual edict, the laws of the people, and the decrees of the senate, succeeded to the authority of the text; and the text was abandoned, as a useless, though venerable, relic of antiquity. The *Code*, the *Pandects*, and the *Institutes*, were declared to be the legitimate system of civil jurisprudence; they alone were admitted in the tribunals, and they alone were taught in the academies of Rome, Constantinople, and Berytus.

By the common law the text is not a relic of antiquity, useless or venerable or otherwise. It is living law, built on what has gone before, but open to constant renewal.

I said I would give two instances of the common law's processes in action: the sovereignty of Parliament, and the judicial review jurisdiction. There are many others in the field of private law. They include the evolution of the law of negligence into a coherent whole; and the recent movement of the law of defamation towards a principled arena of privacy and free speech. But I am concerned with the common law and state power, to which my two instances are most germane. I turn to the first: the sovereignty of Parliament.

[7] *Ibid.*

The Sovereignty of Parliament

Whether or not the doctrine of parliamentary sovereignty should be ascribed to decisions of the courts has been a matter of academic contention.[8] I am not here concerned to enter into the substance of this debate, though I favour the view that sovereignty is a common law construct.[9] It is enough for my present purpose to recognise that the reach or scope of the doctrine has been honed and conditioned by the common law. Sir Edward Coke considered that the judges would not give effect to an Act of Parliament if it lacked all reason, though the meaning of his famous *dictum* to that effect in *Dr Bonham's Case*[10] in 1610 has been disputed. Plainly, moreover, Coke's view is far from the modern law. Here is Blackstone, writing of course in the eighteenth century:

> If the parliament will positively enact a thing to be done which is unreasonable, I know of no power that can control it: and the examples alleged in support of this sense of the rule do none of them prove, that where the main object of a statute is unreasonable the judges are at liberty to reject it; for that were to set the judicial power above that of the legislature, which would be subversive of all government.

[8] The history and philosophy of legislative supremacy cannot sensibly be studied without recourse to Jeffrey Goldsworthy's work, *The Sovereignty of Parliament: History and Philosophy* (Oxford University Press, 1999), to which I refer further below.

[9] My judgment in the so-called 'Metric Martyrs' case, *Thoburn* [2003] QB 151, to which I will refer in Lecture III, touches on this.

[10] 8 Co. Rep. 107; 77 Eng. Rep. 638.

This has been received doctrine; most famously, I suppose, expounded by Dicey in *An Introduction to the Study of the Law of the Constitution*. But this received doctrine has come under question in recent years. Here is Lord Hope's well-known observation in *Jackson* v. *Attorney General*,[11] the challenge to the hunting legislation, in 2005:

> Our constitution is dominated by the sovereignty of Parliament. But parliamentary sovereignty is no longer, if it ever was, absolute. It is not uncontrolled in the sense referred to by Lord Birkenhead LC in *McCawley* v. *The King* [1920] AC 691, 720. It is no longer right to say that its freedom to legislate admits of no qualification whatever. Step by step, gradually but surely, the English principle of the absolute legislative sovereignty of Parliament which Dicey derived from Coke and Blackstone is being qualified.

The reference to the principle's derivation from Coke hardly sits with *Dr Bonham's Case* – but set that aside. The pressures on legislative sovereignty have, of course, largely come from the law of the European Union and the law of fundamental rights, greatly influenced but not wholly determined by the passage of the European Convention on Human Rights into our domestic law by force of the Human Rights Act 1998. What is important for my purpose is that these pressures are managed and contained by the common law; and that is only made possible by the common law's process of continuous self-correction, at once allowed and restrained by the four

[11] [2006] 1 AC 262, para. 104.

methods which I have described. This is the truth behind Lord Hope's reference to a gradual evolution, step by step.

As regards sovereignty and the European Union, as I put it in the *Thoburn* case in 2002,[12] 'the courts have found their way through the *impasse* seemingly created by two supremacies, the supremacy of European law and the supremacy of Parliament'. I will describe the process in Lecture III.

As for sovereignty and the law of fundamental rights, it is of course well known that the Human Rights Act 1998 does not purport to confer on the courts any power of review of legislation. Formally at least, it leaves the sovereignty of Parliament intact; though the requirement of section 3 that Acts of Parliament are to be read compatibly with the Convention rights 'so far as it is possible to do so' gives a powerful steer to the practical impact of legislation. But the common law does this independently and was doing it before the 1998 Act had effect. In *Ex parte Pierson*[13] in 1998, Lord Browne-Wilkinson said:

> A power conferred by Parliament in general terms is not to be taken to authorise the doing of acts by the donee of the power which adversely affect the legal rights of the citizen or the basic principles on which the law of the United Kingdom is based unless the statute conferring the power makes it clear that such was the intention of Parliament.

One may compare statements by Lord Hoffmann in *Ex parte Simms*[14] in 1999, and as it happens by myself in *Ex parte Witham*[15] in 1997:

[12] [2003] QB 151, para. 60. [13] [1998] AC 539, paras. 575C–D.
[14] [2000] 2 AC 115. [15] [1998] 2 WLR 849.

> In the unwritten legal order of the British State, at a time when the common law continues to accord a legislative supremacy to Parliament, the notion of a constitutional right can ... inhere only in this proposition, that the right in question cannot be abrogated by the State save by specific provision in an Act of Parliament.[16]

In all this jurisprudence, as with the Human Rights Act, the sovereignty of Parliament is formally left intact. But the common law, quite aside from the Human Rights Act, has increasingly come to recognise that the modern British state has need of constitutional rights, and that the bland equality of all statutes belongs to an earlier age. That is of high importance for our understanding of the nature of legislative supremacy. I will have more to say about sovereignty's evolution at the hands of the common law when I come shortly to what I have called the constitutional balance; this is at the core of this Lecture. At this stage I offer sovereignty as my first instance of change effected through the common law's processes in action.

Judicial Review

These refinements of legislative supremacy march alongside the maturing of the judicial review jurisdiction, my second instance of the common law's processes in action. Now, as is well known, judicial review has its origins in the mediaeval prerogative writs of certiorari, prohibition and mandamus. Prohibition was the oldest. Although at various times some

[16] *Ibid.* para. 13.

of the writs were issued out of the Court of Common Pleas and the Court of Chancery, pre-eminently they were remedies of the Court of King's Bench; they were the means by which the King's Bench kept other courts within the limits of their jurisdiction. At length the power to issue the prerogative writs devolved to the High Court upon the coming into effect of the Judicature Act 1873. Cases decided in the years after the Judicature Act reflect the earlier primacy of the King's Bench over inferior courts; but sometimes their language looks forward to the constitutional character of modern judicial review. Thus, in 1882 in *R (on the Prosecution of the Penarth Local Board)* v. *Local Government Board*,[17] Brett LJ stated:

> [M]y view of the power of prohibition at the present day is that the Court should not be chary of exercising it, and that wherever the legislature entrusts to any body of persons other than to the superior Courts the power of imposing an obligation upon individuals, the Courts ought to exercise as widely as they can the power of controlling those bodies of persons if those persons admittedly attempt to exercise powers beyond the powers given to them by Act of Parliament.

Scroll forward 106 years to 1988, and in *Ex parte Vijayatunga*,[18] Simon Brown J was able to assert a general principle:

> Judicial review is the exercise of the court's inherent power at common law to determine whether action is lawful or not; in a word to uphold the rule of law. (343E–F)

[17] (1882) 10 QBD 309, 321. [18] [1988] QB 322.

Judicial review now constitutes the primary means of confining state power within its proper legal limits. Every public body except the Queen in Parliament is subject to its jurisdiction. As a means of controlling lower courts, it has all but disappeared, being largely replaced by systems of statutory appeals. Now it is primarily directed at executive government, national and local. Its modern incarnation, born of the ancient prerogative writs, is a striking product of the common law's process of continuous self-correction.

In recent years there has been a lively academic controversy upon the question whether the judicial review jurisdiction is no more than the enforcer of the *ultra vires* doctrine, that is to say, the means by which the law restrains every public body within the powers actually or presumably conferred upon it by Parliament.[19] On this view every public law doctrine – fairness, reasonableness, good faith – is ultimately founded upon the will of Parliament. Even though the statute in question contains no express prescription of such disciplines, still they are the mandate of the legislature, albeit implicit. Even judicial review of powers exercised under the Royal Prerogative, thus owing nothing on the face of it to any statute, obtains its legitimacy from Parliament's implicit permission.

I cannot do justice to this debate in this Lecture. But I should say that I have always opposed the *ultra vires* view of

[19] There is a considerable literature. A good deal of it is referred to in the section 4 on 'The Doctrine of *Ultra Vires*' in H. W. R. Wade and C. F. Forsyth, *Administrative Law* (9th edn, Oxford, Clarendon Press, 2004), ch. 2, pp. 35–42, esp. pp. 38–40 and note 77). Wade and Forsyth take the pro-*ultra vires* view.

the judicial review jurisdiction: first, because it is a fiction, and with nothing of Plato's Noble Lie about it. The discipline of the common law's principles is in no sense the creature of the legislature, and the conventional appeal, so often to be found in the cases, to the will of Parliament does not make it so. Secondly, however, since the *ultra vires* doctrine of judicial review places everything in the hands of Parliament, it implies a power in Parliament to override any restraining principle of civilised government: any fundamental constitutional protection which the common law might evolve for the protection of the people. But at a certain distant point, complicity with this kind of absolutism would call in question the judge's loyalty to his judicial oath. Jeffrey Goldsworthy suggests[20] that in 'an extraordinary situation' judges might decide to disobey statute 'on the ground that their legal duty is overridden by a moral duty to disobey'. He says:

> [w]hat judges might be morally entitled or even bound to do in an extraordinary emergency may differ from what they are legally authorised to do. It does not follow from the fact that judges must decide for themselves whether or not they can enforce a statute with a clear conscience, that if they decide they cannot do so, they have authority to hold that the statute is legally invalid.[21]

But this appeal to morals as a refuge from law will not do. What would 'legal validity' mean in such a situation? Not only that – the disobedient judge would not merely be following his

[20] Goldsworthy, *The Sovereignty of Parliament*, n. 8 above, p. 10.

[21] *Ibid.* p. 264.

conscientious predilections. He would be acting out of loyalty to his judicial oath: his constitutional, and therefore his legal duty. If his proposed action, however conscientious, were contrary to his oath rather than required by it, his duty would be different: it would be to resign his office.

The Constitutional Balance

The *ultra vires* debate and the duty of the judges brings me to what I have called the constitutional balance. The sovereignty of Parliament itself only has life by means of the common law's methods. The judicial ascertainment of an Act's meaning, and the judicial elaboration of substantive principle, are indissolubly interwoven. This meeting of Parliament and judges is the constitutional balance. It is at the core of my thesis in this Lecture: by force of the common law, efficacy is allowed but oppression is forbidden to the power of the state, and this is achieved by a benign *continuum* of developing law.

Let me turn, then, to the constitutional balance. The starting-point is that sovereignty is not merely concerned with the possibly jejune question whether Parliament may pass any legislation whatever and have it obeyed. In practice, sovereignty can only be understood by reference to the condition on which Parliament's legislation is given effect. I do not mean mere points of manner and form. I mean the need for Parliament's law to be interpreted – mediated – to the people. I said above that an Act of Parliament is words on a page; only the common law gives it life. This truism (banality, even) holds the clue to the reality of the constitutional balance.

It is obvious that an Act of Parliament, words on a page, can have no effect without an interpreter. There is an arresting passage in Plato's dialogue the *Phaedrus*, in which Socrates, who never wrote down any of his philosophy, is discussing the written word:

> Writing, Phaedrus, has this strange quality, and is very like painting; for the creatures of painting stand like living beings, but if one asks them a question, they preserve a solemn silence. And so it is with written words; you might think they spoke as if they had intelligence, but if you question them, wishing to know about their sayings, they always say only one and the same thing. And every word, when it is written, is bandied about, alike among those who understand and those who have no interest in it, and it knows not to whom to speak or not to speak; when ill-treated or unjustly reviled it always needs its father to help it; for it has no power to protect or help itself.[22]

There is a strange affinity, I think, between this passage and some lines in TS Eliot's *Burnt Norton*:

> Words strain,
> Crack and sometimes break, under the burden,
> Under the tension, slip, slide, perish,
> Decay with imprecision, will not stay in place,
> Will not stay still.

In the *Phaedrus* '[e]very word, when it is written, is bandied about' ('rolled around', I think, is a better translation of the

[22] Plato, *Phaedrus*, 275d–e (H. N. Fowler (trans.), Loeb Classical Library).

Greek verb[23]); in *Burnt Norton* '[w]ords will not stay in place, will not stay still'. I think the insight is that the power of the written word is never on the page, but always in the mind of the reader. The page does not communicate itself. The words will only stay in place, stay still, when they are interpreted.

For literature, the reader's own interpretation may suffice. But not for law. Statutory text has to be controlled by impartial and independent judicial authority. In *Cart and others*[24] in 2009, I said:

> 37. . . . The interpreter's role cannot be filled by the legislature or the executive: for in that case they or either of them would be judge in their own cause, with the ills of arbitrary government which that would entail. Nor, generally, can the interpreter be constituted by the public body which has to administer the relevant law: for in that case the decision-makers would write their own laws. The interpreter must be impartial, independent both of the legislature and of the persons affected by the texts' application, and authoritative – accepted as the last word, subject only to any appeal. Only a court can fulfil the role.
>
> 38. If the meaning of statutory text is not controlled by such a judicial authority, it would at length be degraded to nothing more than a matter of opinion. Its scope and content would become muddied and unclear.

In our jurisdiction, the judicial authority which interprets statute is the common law. Its fourfold method is therefore integral not only to the common law's own creations outside statute, but also to the interpretation of all our legislation.

[23] κυλινδειται. [24] [2009] EWHC Admin 3052, [2010] 2 WLR 1012.

To understand the importance of this, there are two points to be made. (1) What in the *patois* of the law are called rules of construction or interpretation are as normative, as full of value, as any substantive legal principle. The construction of statutes is not merely an exercise in grammar or syntax. It is full of presumptions and rules which reflect substantive values: the presumption against retrospectivity; the rule that taxing and criminal statutes must be interpreted strictly (though the first of these, relating to tax, may be on the march today); the rule that fundamental rights may only be interfered with by express words or necessary implication. (2) There are differences in kind between decision-making by the courts and decision-making by the legislature. The common law is gradual, but legislation is immediate. Parliament's law is not an evolutive or gradual process at all. Parliament can only make black-letter law. Though sometimes there are paving Acts that prepare the way for more to come; there may be provisions allowing Secretaries of State to go on and make detailed regulations; there may be long delays before the Act comes into force; and there may be (there very often are) amendments and re-amendments – still, generally, a statute is complete when it is passed, like the goddess Athene born from the head of Zeus. And it may be extinguished as completely, by another statute. Parliament's very sovereignty dooms its products to a transient, at least a precarious, existence. Whereas the courts hone and refine principles over time, the legislature creates new regimes at every turn. It may, and often does, reinvent the wheel. The courts do not. Courts and Parliament both make new lamps, but the courts make new lamps from old.

These two circumstances – (1) that judicial interpretation is evaluative, not merely grammatical, and (2) that the common law is gradual, but legislation is immediate – describe the interdependence between the judiciary and the political arms of government. Their contrasting methodologies are apt and necessary to their respective constitutional tasks. Parliament's black-letter law puts the policy of democratic government onto the statute book. The courts' refinement of principle, through the common law's fourfold method, mediates the policy to the people. It provides as close a fit as possible between the policy of Parliament and values – reason, fairness and the presumption of liberty – which over time have come to reflect and moderate the temper of the people. This is what I mean by the condition on which legislation is given effect: the need for statute to be mediated to the people by the common law. It recalls the words of Sir Edward Coke: 'the surest construction of a statute is by the rule and reason of the common law'.[25]

But there is a third point to be made. A better understanding of the effect of this symbiosis of courts and Parliament calls in question the cliché that Parliament makes law and judges interpret it. What do we mean by 'interpret'? I have said that our rules of interpretation are as normative, as full of value, as any substantive legal principle. But that is not a complete account of the impact of the common law upon legislation. The task of construing an Act of Parliament has,

[25] 1 Co. Inst. 272b, quoted in T. R. S. Allan, *Law, Liberty and Justice: The Legal Foundations of British Constitutionalism* (Oxford, Clarendon Press, 1993), p. 15.

of course, to be performed in a whole series of legal contexts. Sometimes, indeed, it involves little more than grammar or syntax. But sometimes interpretation is the engine of deep constitutional principle. This was true of the seminal cases of *Anisminic*[26] and *Padfield*[27] in the 1960s. It is true of the cases which moderate parliamentary sovereignty, and those which fitted judicial review to confine public power within the limits set by the law.

More than this: the interpretation of statutes cannot be seen as an isolated exercise. Recall Lord Diplock's threefold classification of the grounds of judicial review in the *CCSU* case: illegality, irrationality and procedural impropriety. Superficially one might suppose that statutory construction is only involved in the first of these, illegality. But a judgment whether a public decision taken under statutory powers is irrational (or nowadays, disproportionate), or procedurally unfair, may just as surely depend on the correct construction of the statute which confers the relevant power.

The reality is that the judicial ascertainment of an Act's meaning, and the judicial elaboration of substantive principle, are indissolubly interwoven. The slogan – Parliament makes law and the judges interpret it – is a coarse over-simplification. The Act's meaning gives vital colour to what may reasonably be done under its powers; and what is reasonable – or fair or just – gives vital colour to the Act's meaning. This mutuality is at the core of the relation between the legislature and the judiciary. To it the legislature brings its sovereign power to make black-letter law. The judiciary brings the fourfold methodology of the

[26] [1969] 2 AC 147. [27] [1968] AC 997.

common law. The practical relation between the two is constituted by three propositions: (1) judicial interpretation is evaluative, not merely grammatical; (2) the common law is gradual, but legislation is immediate; (3) interpretation and the elaboration of principle are indissoluble. These three propositions involve a compromise between the immediacy of political will and the gradual processes of the common law. They create the constitutional balance. By this means statute law and government policy are alike delivered to the people through the prism of reason, fairness and the presumption of liberty, and the legislature is allowed efficacy but forbidden oppression. It is, I think, noteworthy that article 5 of the French Civil Code provides that 'judges are not permitted to adjudicate on cases before them by way of statement of general principle or statutory construction'. As Lord Sumption has said,[28] '[t]his means that judges may only formulate principles applicable to the particular facts before them. They may not purport to lay down general rules which would apply in any other case. That would be classified as an essentially legislative function'.

The daily diet of the Administrative Court does not, of course, consist in challenges to the validity of primary legislation. Rather, the standard case of judicial review involves an assault on the exercise of statutory discretion, often by central government. Still, the constitutional balance is at the heart of it, for it colours and informs the court's view of the legislation which grants the discretion. And in such cases this balance imposes a discipline not only on the public law defendant, but

[28] Twenty-seventh Sultan Azlan Shah Lecture, Kuala Lumpur, 20 November 2013.

also on the court itself; for it is a necessary condition of the constitutional balance that the court respects the powers which Parliament delegates to the officers of government. The obvious truth that the judges are not the authors of statutory powers or government policy conceals a more subtle reality: it is only because they stand at a distance from the rancour and populism of the political function that they possess the authority to create and evolve dispassionate constitutional principles. It is thus an authority which depends on restraint. This aspect of the constitutional balance is under pressure from the burgeoning of human rights laws, which may provoke the judges to exceed their proper place. I will consider this in Lecture III, 'The Common Law and Europe'.

Sovereignty Revisited

Let me return to the sovereignty of Parliament, whose nature has to be understood in light of the constitutional balance. For all the reasons I have given, the judicial interpretation of statutes is a condition on which Parliament's legislation is given effect. I think it is a compulsory condition. In 2009 in the case of *Cart and others*,[29] to which I referred earlier, I said this:

> If the meaning of statutory text is not controlled by such a judicial authority, it would at length be degraded to nothing more than a matter of opinion. Its scope and content would become muddied and unclear. Public bodies would not, by means of the judicial review jurisdiction,

[29] [2009] EWHC Admin 3052, [2010] 2 WLR 1012, para. 38.

> be kept within the confines of their powers prescribed by statute. The very effectiveness of statute law, Parliament's law, requires that none of these things happen. Accordingly, as it seems to me, the need for such an authoritative judicial source cannot be dispensed with by Parliament. This is not a denial of legislative sovereignty, but an affirmation of it: as is the old rule that Parliament cannot bind itself. The old rule means that successive Parliaments are always free to make what laws they choose; that is one condition of Parliament's sovereignty. The requirement of an authoritative judicial source for the interpretation of law means that Parliament's statutes are always effective; that is another.

I should say that in the same case in the Supreme Court, Lord Phillips observed:[30]

> The proposition that parliamentary sovereignty requires Parliament to respect the power of the High Court to subject the decisions of public authorities, including courts of limited jurisdiction, to judicial review is controversial. Hopefully the issue will remain academic.

I am not quite sure why we should hope that this issue will remain academic. The requirement of independent statutory interpretation by the judges applying the principles of the common law is not a desirable extra, nor the fifth wheel of the coach – it is integral to the constitutional balance. Without it, the constitution stands on one leg without a crutch.

[30] [2012] 1 AC 663, para. 73.

There is a little more to say. I think that contemporary debate upon the subject of legislative supremacy possesses altogether too sharp an edge. On the one hand, Trevor Allan, whose writings mark him as something of a champion of the common law,[31] roundly concludes that the sovereignty of Parliament is a mistake, because it is in conflict with the common law's fundamental principles: 'the traditional role of the common law in defence of justice and liberty ... is radically inconsistent with a notion of unlimited legislative supremacy'.[32] On the other hand, Jeffrey Goldsworthy[33] no less roundly proclaims the truth and the wisdom of legislative supremacy. He states that[34] 'genuine and lasting respect for the rights of others cannot be imposed by judicial *fiat*: it is most likely to emerge from the dialogue and compromise that characterise politics in a democracy'. And this marches, I think, with positions taken by Jeremy Waldron concerning disagreements about rights.[35] Waldron disapproves of 'American-style' judicial review of legislation.[36]

I have come to think that this polarised debate, sovereignty or no sovereignty, misses the reality of our common law constitution. I can see that there may appear to be an unbridgeable divide between the views of common law constitutionalists such as Trevor Allan and the loyalists of

[31] See in particular, *Law, Liberty and Justice: The Legal Foundations of British Constitutionalism* (Oxford, Clarendon Press, 1993).

[32] *Ibid.* p. 17.

[33] Goldsworthy, *The Sovereignty of Parliament*, n. 8 above, esp. pp. 247–77.

[34] *Ibid.* p. 263.

[35] *Law and Disagreement* (Oxford University Press, 1999).

[36] *Ibid.* p. 15.

sovereignty such as Jeffrey Goldsworthy. The pull towards sovereignty is that someone has to be Master, and the Master should be the people's representatives. The pull against it is that the all-powerful democracy may trample over fundamental rights and freedoms. But the issue need not be seen in the contours of so stark a contrast. Sovereignty may readily acknowledge practical limits, accepted in the name of reason, fairness and the presumption of liberty. They are the gifts of the common law. This is key to a proper understanding of parliamentary sovereignty. It marches with the reasoning of John McGarry of Edge Hill University in a very interesting recent article in the *Journal of the Society of Legal Scholars*.[37] Legislative supremacy is not a doctrine set in stone. It is an evolving legal construct: a principle, not a rule. Granted that, at the least, the reach or scope of the doctrine has been honed and conditioned by the common law, we should understand that the common law's fourfold method applies to its development as well as to that of any other legal sphere.

Where a clash seems to loom between the claims of the sovereign legislature and those of deep individual rights, it will time after time be resolved by recourse to interpretation, and therefore by the methods of the common law. The theoretical possibility that the judges might have to disapply an Act of Parliament lies at the end of a very long road marked failure – a place where the legislature would have lost its integrity. There are, of course, some areas where there is less scope for this qualifying power of the judges than in others – national defence in an emergency, macro-economic policy. The reality

[37] 'The Principle of Parliamentary Sovereignty' (2012) **32**(4) *Legal Studies*.

of legislative sovereignty is that it is variable. It is bigger in some places than in others. The debate about supremacy is hung on a spike of absolutism, of all or nothing. But the constitutional balance, the compromise between the immediacy of political will and the gradual processes of the common law, ought to tell us that the power of the legislature is far more nuanced. The common law's necessary mediation of statute gives us the moderate and orderly development of state power; and so the legislature is allowed efficacy but forbidden oppression.

At the beginning I identified two contemporary threats to the constitutional balance. The first is that present-day fears, real and imagined, of the grip of extremism exert an unwanted, perhaps dangerous, pressure on the moderate liberality of the common law. As I said, I will explain and confront this in Lecture II, 'The Common Law and Extremism'. The second is that the actual or perceived effects of law made in Europe upon our domestic system may undermine virtues of the common law: its catholicity and its restraint. I will explain and confront this in Lecture III, 'The Common Law and Europe'. The importance of these matters does not merely rest in the merits of individual outcomes. They are examples of the challenge which the common law constitution will always face, a challenge born of its very openness. Because our law is constantly renewed by the force of fresh examples; because it reflects and moderates the temper of the people as age succeeds age; because it builds on the experience of ordinary struggles, its principles will be buffeted by events. In difficult times the legislature and the executive will press hard upon the common law's moderating force in the search for political solutions. And there will be places and times when that moderating force will have to give ground. The challenge in the end is simply expressed: it is to keep the constitutional balance, and thus to give the principles of the common law – reason, fairness and the presumption of liberty – as big a space as possible. Easily said; harder to do. It needs intelligence, certainly. But it needs courage and imagination as well. The task is difficult because the principles of the common law, which make the constitutional balance, are themselves constantly being reworked through the common law's distinctive methods. But their inheritance is not a mere chameleon. The common law constitution, fashioned by the balance I have described, confers a great political gift: the harmony of freedom and justice, and therefore the tranquillity of the state. We owe it both pride and vigilance.

LECTURE II

The Common Law and Extremism

In Lecture I, I described the constitutional balance between law and government, between the judicial and political arms of the state. The constitutional balance involves a compromise between the immediacy of political will and the gradual processes of the common law. It works in practice through the medium of three truths: (1) judicial interpretation is evaluative, not merely grammatical; (2) the common law is gradual, but legislation is immediate; (3) interpretation and the elaboration of principle are indissoluble. By means of the constitutional balance statute law and government policy are both delivered to the people through the prism of reason, fairness and the presumption of liberty, and the legislature is allowed efficacy but forbidden oppression. The result is our possession of a great political gift, the harmony of freedom and justice, and therefore the tranquillity of the state.

However, I identified two contemporary threats to the constitutional balance. The first, the subject of this Lecture, is that present-day fears, real and imagined, of the grip of extremism exert an unwanted, perhaps dangerous, pressure on the moderate liberality of the common law. This threat, and the threat I shall describe in Lecture III, are examples of the challenge which the common law constitution will always face, a challenge born of its very openness. Because our law is constantly renewed by the force of fresh examples; because it reflects and moderates the temper of the people as age succeeds age; because it builds on the experience of ordinary struggles, its principles, and therefore the constitutional balance, will always be buffeted by events. In difficult times the legislature and the executive will press hard upon the common law's moderating force in the search for political solutions. And there will be places and times when that moderating force will have to give ground. The challenge is to keep the constitutional balance.

In this Lecture, extremism and the perception of it are the context of the challenge. Extremism tests the mettle of the good constitution because it presses on the limits of tolerance and of due process. I will try and show how the common law meets, or ought to meet, this threat to its moderate liberality.

The Nature of Extremism

I will start by seeking to explain what I mean by extremism. I have found this to be much more elusive than it seems. While it is unproductive to get bogged down in definitions, I must devote much of the lecture to an effort to unravel the nature of the beast.

The sense which I will ascribe to extremism has two elements. These are, first, an unquestioning commitment to a comprehensive political or religious doctrine by which society should be ordered or re-ordered. The second element is the believer's no less unquestioning commitment to an overriding agenda for the translation of his doctrine into reality. By overriding, I mean an agenda whose fulfilment the extremist believes justified whatever the cost, in blood or anything else.

So there are two elements, the doctrine and the agenda. Between them they constitute the extremist paradigm. There will be softer cases, where the believer's commitment to the doctrine or the agenda is not quite unquestioning, or where either the doctrine or the agenda admits of some give and take; and perhaps more often still, where the believer's agenda is not so grandiose, but amounts only (as if that were not enough) to a relish for casual thuggery against perceived non-believers.

There are, of course, other very different cases which as a matter of language may well merit the name extremism, but where we would have no inclination to condemn: most likely the opposite. The Amish people of Pennsylvania, who eschew all manner of modern conveniences, may be called extremist. They are kindly and peaceful. Those who have been prepared to die for their faith – to be martyrs – may also be so described; though so-called martyrs, murderers whose purpose is to take others, innocent bystanders, with them, are to be excoriated as extremists as I mean the term.

My description of the extremist's doctrine – an unquestioning commitment to a comprehensive political or religious doctrine by which society should be ordered or re-ordered – is in one sense a surprising touchstone for extremism, for it says nothing about the *content* of an extremist doctrine. But it seems to me that the public vice of extremism – that is, the vice which concerns the law – does not rest in the moral shortcomings of this or that personal belief system, but rather in the extremist's unquestioning devotion to its fulfilment: its fulfilment whatever the cost, as I have said, in blood or anything else. This is what turns his doctrine into an agenda for action. So the focus is very much on the agenda.

However, the content of the extremist's doctrine is very important. An agenda of the kind an extremist entertains is not fuelled by just any kind of belief system, any kind of doctrine. Only a doctrine that is deaf to other voices will do it – only a doctrine which, in the mind of the believer, possesses such a towering and unarguable truth that its vindication by whatever it takes is obviously and conspicuously justified. A belief in the tolerance of other views cannot therefore qualify as such a doctrine, let alone a positive approbation of the freedom of the individual. Beliefs of that kind involve give and take, a respect for different choices, a readiness to hear new arguments, to consider facts which might lead to a change of mind. The extremist view, whatever its content, brooks no compromise. The believer entertains an ineffable confidence in his own rightness. So although, on the view I take, the distinct vice of extremism is not simply the vice of vile opinions but rests in the believer's unquestioning commitment to the doctrine he embraces, generally it is only a vile opinion that will fuel so driven a commitment: uncompromising, absolutist and therefore brutal. The nature of the doctrine, and the extremist's unquestioning devotion to its fulfilment, feed off each other.

Euthyphro's Dilemma

This vice, the believer's unquestioning commitment, is illuminated by a famous dilemma. It is to be found in Plato's dialogue, *Euthyphro*. This is one of the dialogues that deal with Socrates' trial, condemnation and death in 399 BC at the hands of the restored Athenian democracy. Socrates says to his young friend Euthyphro, for whom the dialogue is named:

> Just consider this question: is that which is holy loved by the gods because it is holy, or is it holy because it is loved by the gods?[1]

Euthyphro's dilemma has been recycled many times in debates about religious, moral and political authority. In the religious context it may be rephrased thus:

> Are moral acts willed by God because they are good, or are they good because they are willed by God?

In the political context, we may restate the dilemma in this way:

> Are laws or policies willed by the state because they are good, or are they good because they are willed by the state?

The dilemma provides a striking insight into two opposing views of value. The first is that the ascertainment of what is good is a function of man's reason – and, no doubt, other gifts of humanity: imagination, the capacity for love, the fact that he lives in community with others of his kind. I will call this the critical view, the right arm of Euthyphro's dilemma. The second is that goodness is an axiom, a given, dictated by an external force. I will call this the uncritical view, the wrong arm of Euthyphro's dilemma. The extremist always, or nearly always, takes the uncritical view. His values are derived from someone else's utterance, man or god, an utterance which he treats, uncritically, as a command to be obeyed. There is one exception – a different kind of extremist. This is the megalomaniac, who thinks that goodness flows from his own utterance. But he also thinks that everyone else should

[1] *Euthyphro*, 10A (H. N. Fowler (trans.), Loeb Classical Library).

agree with him; so that for them, for all of them, goodness remains an axiom, a given, dictated by an external force – himself. Tyrants down the ages have belonged to this category.

There is a logical difficulty with the uncritical view, the wrong arm of Euthyphro's dilemma. It commits what is sometimes called the naturalistic fallacy, or Hume's Law: you cannot derive an *ought* from an *is*.[2] The uncritical view essentially consists, as I have said, in a command theory of morals: you are bound to act according to the dictates of someone else. But the fact that X commands you to do Y cannot of itself entail that you should do it. There must always be a higher premise, from which the duty to obey X may be supplied; but of course X cannot himself provide the premise.

The uncritical view also presents a severe practical difficulty, perhaps more important than the logical one for an understanding of extremism in the world of events. If you take your morals entirely and uncritically from an external source, your own reason cannot moderate them; they are simply given to you. You cannot tailor your judgement in the light of experience; you cannot discard a failed principle in favour of something better, more humane. There is no scope for a self-correcting discipline. A doctrine, a belief system, arrived at uncritically as an act of supposed obedience, is of its nature prone to unreason. It is like a body with no immune system. As I have said, the nature of the extremist's doctrine – uncompromising, absolutist and therefore brutal – and the extremist's unquestioning devotion to its fulfilment, and

[2] See David Hume, *A Treatise of Human Nature*, Bk III, pt. I, s. 1, at 469; compare G. E. Moore, *Principia Ethica*, 9–10.

therefore his agenda, feed off each other. It is largely because the extremist is on the wrong arm of Euthyphro's dilemma.

Religion

Religion is fertile territory for the uncritical view, because generally it depends on faith or revelation. The core of some religious positions consists in absolute obedience to divine command, revealed in the pages of a Holy Book whose literal truth is accepted without question. Such instances exemplify the abdication of the power to think for oneself, as Charles Freeman put it in *The Closing of the Western Mind.*[3] Freeman cites the words of a Jesuit authority, quoted in William James' celebrated study, *The Varieties of Religious Experience*:[4]

> One of the great consolations of the monastic life is the assurance that we have that in obeying we can commit no fault. The Superior may commit a fault in commanding you to do this or that, but you are certain that you commit no fault so long as you obey, because God will only ask you if you have duly performed what orders you received, and if you can furnish a clear account in that respect, you are absolved entirely ... The moment what you did was done obediently, God wipes it out of your account and charges it to the Superior. So that Saint Jerome well exclaimed 'Oh, holy and blessed security by which one becomes almost impeccable'.

[3] (Pimlico, 2003), ch. 16, p. 256.

[4] (Longmans, Green & Co., 1902), Lecture XIII, p. 312. (The book reproduces James' Gifford Lectures delivered at Edinburgh in 1901–1902.)

One may compare the Muslim visitor to the House of Commons described by Bernard Lewis in *What Went Wrong? Western Impact and Middle Eastern Response*:[5]

> In the first extant Muslim account of the British House of Commons, written by a visitor who went to England at the end of the eighteenth century, the writer expresses his astonishment at the fate of a people who, unlike the Muslims, did not have a divine revealed law, and were therefore reduced to the pitiable expedient of enacting their own laws.

Despite these dismal instances, the critical view, the right arm of Euthyphro's dilemma, has surfaced in the history of the West in sometimes surprising and unpromising circumstances. In AD 382 the Emperor Gratian removed the Altar of Victory from the Senate House in Rome. He did so in the name of the Christian religion; for the Altar, before which for generations the senators had sworn their allegiance to a succession of new Emperors, marked obeisance to the old gods. Aurelius Symmachus, the Prefect of Rome, petitioned Gratian's half-brother Valentinian II for the Altar's restoration. Valentinian had made some attempt to restrain the despoiling of pagan temples in Rome. Symmachus said:

> That which all venerate should in fairness be accounted as one. We look on the same stars, the heaven is common to us all, the same world surrounds us. What matters it by what arts each of us seeks for truth? We cannot arrive by one and the same path at so great a secret.

[5] (Phoenix, 2002), p. 127.

But Valentinian refused the petition at the insistence of Ambrose, Bishop of Milan, who appealed to him:

> not to give your answer in accordance with this heathen petition, or sign your name to such an answer, for it would be sacrilegious.

What Aurelius Symmachus said resonates today.[6] We are less sure of rock-solid verities. It was the great American judge, Learned Hand, speaking of freedom, who said[7] that '[t]he spirit of liberty is the spirit which is not too sure that it is right'. Sure or unsure, there is no compulsory road to a compulsory truth.

In light of these reflections, Euthyphro's dilemma – or the wrong arm of it, the uncritical view – poses, I think, a particular challenge for decent religion. The devout would certainly proclaim an unquestioning commitment to their faith – their doctrine. And those who place a paramount importance upon the words of their holy text may very well be on the wrong arm of Euthyphro's dilemma, which bears the scars of extremism as I have described it. But I have neither arrogance nor ambition to assault religion as such. There are too many mysteries; the first and last things are too great a secret. And, of course, there are many people of the Book who undoubtedly believe their morality comes from God, whose

[6] The discussion in 'Christ and World Faiths', ch. 7 in the Report of the Church of England Doctrine Commission on *The Mystery of Salvation* (Church House Publishing, 1995) shows as much.

[7] In a speech in 1944 in Central Park, New York, at the annual 'I Am an American Day' event, where newly naturalised citizens swore the Pledge of Allegiance. The speech brought him a national reputation for wisdom that lasted until the end of his life.

attitude to their fellow humans is moderate, thoughtful and caring – the opposite of extremist.

I think that the religious – at any rate the Christian religious, and I hope the logic may apply generally – have at least two possible recourses against the perils of the wrong arm of Euthyphro's dilemma. There is the apophatic tradition, favoured in the Eastern Orthodox Church: God is beyond description or definition. You can only say what he is not – the *via negativa*: in the words of the Athanasian Creed, uncreate, incomprehensible; in the familiar hymn, immortal, invisible. One may compare the fourteenth century English guide to spirituality, *The Cloud of Unknowing*: 'He cannot be comprehended by our intellect or any man's – or any angel's for that matter. For both we and they are created beings. But only to our intellect is he incomprehensible: not to our love'.[8] Or there is the rather more terse comment of Ludwig Wittgenstein at the end of the *Tractatus*: 'What we cannot speak about we must pass over in silence'.[9] When it comes to how he should conduct himself, the apophatic tradition must at least to some degree leave the believer to think for himself.

The second recourse is to the long-established Anglican appeal to the combined wisdom of Scripture, tradition and reason. Richard Hooker, appointed Master of the Temple in 1585 and the first great Anglican theologian, brought this tripartite philosophy to its flourishing. The book for which he is remembered, *The Laws of Ecclesiastical Polity*, is 'a

[8] *The Cloud of Unknowing*, translated into modern English by Clifton Wolters (Penguin Classics, reprinted 1983).

[9] (Pears and McGuinness (trans.)), para. 7.

carefully worked answer to seven Puritan propositions'.[10] Hooker's appeal to tradition and reason, alongside Scripture, begins a journey down a road where far greater rewards are to be found. His view of the Bible was, of course, a sixteenth-century view; he affirmed 'the absolute perfection of Scripture', but this was by no means the same as the Puritan principle. For Hooker, reason was a vital guide to the understanding and the use of Scripture. 'For whatsoever we believe concerning salvation by Christ, although the Scripture be therein the ground of our belief; yet the authority of man is, if we mark it, the key which openeth the door of entrance into the knowledge of the Scripture'.[11]

It is interesting to note that the great English philosopher, John Locke, maintained in *Reasonableness of Christianity as Delivered in the Scriptures* (published in 1695) that the only secure basis of Christianity was its reasonableness. It generated much controversy and criticism. More generally, the Deists of the late seventeenth and eighteenth centuries advocated a form of natural religion whose classical exposition is to be found in John Toland's work *Christianity not Mysterious* of 1696, which argues against revelation and the supernatural altogether. The book was burned by the Irish Parliament in 1697 – the wrong arm of Euthyphro's dilemma.

An approach which gives a proper place to the power of reason allows the derivation of basic moral principles from an external source, the Divinity, but requires an independent and reasoned judgement in the principles' application. To this

[10] McAdoo, *The English Religious Tradition*, p. 111.
[11] *Ecclesiastical Polity*, II, vii, 3.

extent the critical and the uncritical views – the arms of Euthyphro's dilemma – may be said to overlap. I have not the scholarship to know what possibility there may be of applying such a process by analogy to the Koran, the Torah or other non-Christian texts.

I have spoken of religion at some length because, being vulnerable to the wrong arm of Euthyphro's dilemma, it is vulnerable also to the tentacles of extremism. But by no means does it have to succumb. In many traditions it does not do so. And, of course, political extremism is at least as gross a denial of human goodness as the religious variety.

So much, then, about the nature of the extremist's doctrine. What of his agenda? This is where, categorically, the law has to bite; but there is much less to say about it than about the doctrine. The vile cruelty of terrorist crime, state sponsored or otherwise, needs no description from me. However, the egregious case is not the only instance which concerns us, and the justified condemnation of the extremist's agenda carries a danger. The danger is that compulsory law be brought to bear upon the extremist's doctrine, because, and only because, his agenda is vile. This is the pressure on the moderate liberality of the common law which extremism generates: the danger of confusing the doctrine with the agenda. Where is the line to be drawn between the expression of the extremist's doctrine and the execution of his agenda? It is time to turn to the law.

The Law's Place

The starting-point is to see that the critical view of value – the right limb of Euthyphro's dilemma – is inherent in the common law's foundational insights: reason, fairness and the presumption of liberty, enriched and matured by the common law's methods, which I described in Lecture I. I have described the common law's genius: the refinement of principle over time. Its elusive strength is that it reflects and moderates the temper of the people as age succeeds age. It is especially fit for a democratic state, for it builds on the experience of ordinary struggles. It enshrines a cardinal principle of the Enlightenment: that people should think for themselves. It is therefore not a matter of choice that the common law is extremism's enemy. It defines itself as extremism's enemy.

What then is the danger – the pressure point – arising from the question, where is the line to be drawn between the expression of the extremist's doctrine and the execution of his agenda? It is to be found (as I have foreshadowed) in the risk that in choosing measures to counter extremism, the doctrine and the agenda may be confused: the state may take steps to prohibit action not because the action breaches the general law, as where it consists in criminal or tortious conduct, but because the state disapproves of the beliefs behind the action – because, in short, it disapproves of the doctrine.

Now, it is a cardinal, elementary principle of the law of England that everyone is entitled to believe whatever he likes. Queen Elizabeth I is authority for this. You will recall the Black Rubric, one of the instructions appended to the Order for Holy Communion in the Book of Common Prayer. It is in these terms:

> Whereas it is ordained in this office for the Administration of the Lord's Supper, that the Communicants should receive the same kneeling . . . yet, lest the same kneeling

> should by any persons, either out of ignorance and infirmity, or out of malice and obstinacy, be misconstrued and depraved: It is here declared, that thereby no Adoration is intended, or ought to be done, either unto the Sacramental Bread or Wine there bodily received, or unto any Corporal Presence of Christ's natural Flesh and Blood.

The Rubric was composed by Archbishop Cranmer for his second Prayer Book of 1552 – as it happens, the year when Sir Edward Coke was born. It requires the communicant to kneel; but forbids him to worship the bread and wine as if it were Christ's flesh and blood. It is intended to regulate what happens in his head while he is on his knees. Queen Elizabeth I had the Rubric removed. As Sir Francis Bacon tells us, 'She would not make windows into men's souls'. But at the restoration of King Charles II it was restored in the 1662 Prayer Book, and has been the law of the land – the canon law – ever since. It is the only provision I know of remaining in the law of England which forbids free thought.

'She would not make windows into men's souls.' The same principle was stated by Sir Edward Coke (who of course would not have recognised Her late Majesty Queen Elizabeth I as a source of legal precedent[12]). He said: 'No man ecclesiastical or temporal shall be examined upon secret thoughts of his heart or of his secret opinion'. We find what is in effect the same thing in Article 9(1) of the European Convention on Human Rights and Fundamental Freedoms (ECHR): 'Everyone has the right to freedom of thought, conscience and religion'. As is well known the second paragraph

[12] *Prohibitions del Roy* 12 Rep. 64; [1607] EWHC KB J23.

of Article 9 qualifies the right to manifest one's religion or belief; but it by no means curtails the right to adhere to any religion, or entertain any belief. It says: 'Freedom to manifest one's religion or beliefs shall be subject only to such limitations as are prescribed by law and are necessary in a democratic society' – freedom to manifest, not freedom to believe; that is left whole and untouched; and this is the principle of the common law.

It is, no doubt, a hard truth that the right to believe what one likes includes the right to vile or barbarous beliefs. But it must be so. If the state were permitted, in the least degree, to take steps to prevent the citizen from thinking one thing, or to make him think another, it would begin down the road towards mastery over the people; whereas the state must remain the people's servant. That is what marks the difference between a free society and an enslaved people. It means – and this is the point for my present purposes – that the antithesis between the doctrine and the agenda is vital to the workings of the law. The law's response to each of them is, or should be, categorically different from its response to the other. The law must leave the bare doctrine alone. The hope of its extinction rests in precept, example, education (not in what to think, but in how to think) and other resources outwith the compulsory law. The law's business is to prohibit and prevent execution of the agenda, where the agenda violates established legal rule, as for example by incitement to crime. It is not to make windows into men's souls.

Suppressing Doctrine

To many this will seem merely obvious, but it is in some ways a difficult road to follow. Tolerance of the extremist's doctrine encounters difficulties over the doctrine's manifestations. This brings me to the threat to the constitutional balance I described at the start: the risk that fear of the grip of extremism may exert an unwanted, perhaps dangerous, pressure on the moderate liberality of the common law. Should the law forbid the wearing of the *niqab* or the *burkha*? Consider the pressures upon a good answer to such a question. There is a plain danger that the law-givers may be tempted to prohibit a practice not because it is objectively harmful but because they disapprove of the doctrine they think lies behind it. The wearer of the *niqab* or the *burkha*, of course, may or may not be an extremist. Whether she is or not, a proposal to ban her head-dress which is in reality based on nothing but excoriation of her perceived beliefs (and I have heard such things suggested by public figures in the media) confuses the doctrine with the agenda. It is contrary to deep principle. It offends the moderate liberality of the common law.

Possibilities of this kind pose a threat to the constitutional balance because they may weaken the influence of the common law's principles – reason, fairness, the presumption of liberty – on statute law and policy. But our duty is to give these principles as big a space as possible. There may, of course, be justifications for the prohibition in some circumstances of forms of dress, or the display of a badge or symbol, or other outward manifestations of the wearer's belief, whether extremist or not. Public settings in which a person's face needs to be seen (the courtroom, the immigration desk, genuine (not fanciful) considerations of health and safety, reasonable requirements for uniform in school), all these points and others have been much rehearsed in recent debate. The particularity of such issues is not my subject, save to emphasise that solutions to these questions have to be found which do not discriminate between the different faiths or beliefs of the actors concerned. So much is obvious, but it calls up another aspect of the threat to the constitutional balance, pressing on the values of reason and fairness: this is the danger that discrimination may be born out of public cowardice – the fear that some groups may protest more loudly than others. For a public decision-maker to give way to such a fear is a disgrace to his office.

Free Speech

Discriminatory regulation, and the suppression of doctrine as opposed to agenda, may be exemplified by the prohibition of forms of dress or the display of emblems. But the threat to the constitutional balance is all the greater where free speech is prohibited. Here, the common law's presumption of liberty is at its sharpest. The critical view, the right arm of Euthyphro's dilemma, enjoins us to think for ourselves; it tells us that the ascertainment of what is good is a function of man's reason and other gifts of humanity. Plainly, the process cannot operate without the free exchange of ideas. The right arm of Euthyphro's dilemma thus implies a great truth: free expression is morally prior to the content of any man's belief. Accordingly, the supposed falsity of a belief never justifies suppression of its supporters, and the supposed truth of a belief never justifies the suppression of its critics. Note that it cuts both ways. Suppressing doctrine tempts some through hatred of the doctrine; suppressing the doctrine's critics tempts some through a cowardly fear of protest; both are offensive to the moderate liberality of the common law. Both diminish the space given to reason, fairness and the presumption of liberty.

In the realm of free speech, then, there are no masters. The constitutional law of the state must proceed on the footing that the truth or falsity of any belief is irrelevant to the rights of its believers and critics to express their beliefs and criticisms. So we must allow the extremist to entertain his doctrine, and seek to stamp only upon his agenda, where that is unlawful. There are, of course, circumstances in which speech is properly curtailed by the law, most obviously in the present context, when it involves incitement to crime; but then the agenda is the law's target, not the doctrine. I acknowledge it may sometimes be difficult to unravel a case where a speaker merely preaches his doctrine from a case where he preaches action – where he preaches his agenda. In some instances of extremism, the doctrine seems to consist in nothing but the agenda. But we owe a duty to the constitutional balance to distinguish one from the other, where that can be done, and deploy the law accordingly.

Due Process

Now I will turn to another dimension of the threat that extremism offers to the moderate liberality of the common law. As I have said, the law's business is to prohibit and prevent execution of the extremist's agenda, where the agenda violates established legal rule, as for example by incitement to crime or, of course, direct threats to the Queen's peace. Here the challenge to the common law's principles is a familiar one, but notoriously difficult. It consists in the clash of two pressures: the pressure of state security, and the pressure of judicial due process. It arises when the state confronts not imagined, but actual extremism or the threat of it; not the doctrine but, unequivocally, the agenda. Here the state faces a recurrent question: what sanctions are justified against dangerous supporters of terrorism who, however, cannot be brought to trial for want of evidence that can be deployed to support a criminal prosecution?

Though the dilemma is a familiar one, and Parliament and the courts have more than once had to confront it, its constitutional implications are not at once apparent. Consider first the nature of the values in question. On the one hand, the security of the state is a prime duty, some would say the first duty, of government, which may be expected to seek any necessary legislation from Parliament to see that its duty is fulfilled. How can it properly be compromised? On the other hand, detention without trial is, as Sir Winston Churchill said, 'in the highest degree odious'. Lesser forms of restraint such as control orders also affront the value of due process. Due process – no curtailment of liberty without proper proof and fair trial – is surely at the core of a free and just society, part of what defines our excoriation of the terrorist cause.

So far so good: the contrast between security and justice is very easy to state. But now consider the constitutional truth behind it. State security is the duty of government. As I said in Lecture I, national defence is quintessentially an area where there is less scope than in other fields for the qualifying power of the judges. In such an area, the common law voice – the voice of the judges – should presumably be at its softest.

Due process, on the other hand, is the duty of the courts. Its denial offers the plainest offence to the presumption of liberty. Here, then, the common law voice should presumably be at its loudest. So the tension, the contrast, is not merely between two desirable aims, security and justice, but between two arms of the constitution, political and judicial, each with a claim to the louder voice across the divide.

This kind of tension will always arise where one of these constitutional powers steps onto the other's territory. It happens when a treaty (or any other law) seeks to judicialise social and economic rights, and immunise them against the contrary winds of democratic politics. It is exemplified by the requirement that the courts should assess the proportionality of removing alien criminals who claim rights under ECHR Article 8. In these instances the courts are drawn onto political territory. By contrast, statutes which, for example, impose over-rigid criminal sentencing regimes tend the other way; they impose government on the territory of the courts. Moreover, this tension between constitutional powers is exacerbated by the fact that the common law and government have different defining moralities. The law's morality is essentially Kantian, primarily concerned with the justice of individual claims. Government's morality is essentially utilitarian, primarily concerned with strategic outcomes in the public interest.[13] The tension is especially acute in a context like the present, where the turf on either side of the divide so emphatically belongs to one or other of the powers: national security the duty of government, justice the duty of the courts.

[13] I discussed this antithesis in some detail in the Twelfth Sir David Williams Lecture, 'The Good Constitution', Cambridge, 4 May 2012.

But the tranquillity of the state depends upon these powers remaining in balance: the constitutional balance. I said in Lecture I that there will be places and times when the moderating force of the common law will have to give ground, even though the threat to the constitutional balance posed by extremism is directed precisely at the moderate liberality of the common law. Some ground indeed has to be given; there has to be a compromise. But it needs to be understood that such a compromise may disturb the constitutional balance. It needs also to be understood that there must be limits to such a compromise, however difficult they are to find or even to state. All this said, however, the stand-off between justice and security is not absolute; there is common ground. It was articulated by that great common lawyer, Aharon Barak, President of the Supreme Court of Israel from 1995 to 2006, who said this in a case where certain practices of the Israeli security services were subjected to the Supreme Court's scrutiny:

> This is the destiny of democracy, as not all means are acceptable to it and not all practices employed by its enemies are open before it. Although a democracy must often fight with one hand tied behind its back, it nonetheless has the upper hand. Preserving the rule of law and recognition of an individual's liberty constitutes an important component in its understanding of security. At the end of the day they strengthen its spirit and allow it to overcome its difficulties.[14]

[14] See also Prof. Aharon Barak, 'Human Rights and their Limitations: The Role of Proportionality', FLJS Annual Lecture in Law and Society, Rhodes House, Oxford, 4 June 2009.

Faced with the pressing dangers of extremism in this jurisdiction, we have had to find the required and inevitable compromise for our own time. We cannot tie both hands behind democracy's back. We can see the process of compromise being worked through in successive statutes enacting counter-terrorist measures, and the responses of the courts to the curtailment of due process which the measures involve. The ECHR, notably Article 5 which of course provides that '[e]veryone has the right to liberty and security of person', has been the primary shield of due process in the cases.

Let me illustrate the compromise in action. The Anti-terrorism, Crime and Security Act 2001 had by section 23 allowed for the detention without trial of a person certified by the Secretary of State as a suspected international terrorist. In *A and others* v. *Secretary of State*,[15] the House of Lords granted a declaration under section 4 of the Human Rights Act 1998 that section 23 was incompatible with ECHR Articles 5 and 14 as being disproportionate and discriminatory. A new regime to confront the terrorist threat was needed. It was found in the Prevention of Terrorism Act 2005, which repealed section 23 of the previous statute and in the place of detention without trial introduced control orders. A control order might impose severe restrictions on the liberty of the controlled person. On the facts before the House of Lords in *Secretary of State* v. *JJ and others*[16] in October 2007, there was imposed a daily eighteen-hour curfew. The issue in *JJ* was whether the control orders involved a violation of Article 5. In particular the question was whether the effect of the obligations imposed

[15] [2005] 2 AC 68. [16] [2008] 1 AC 385.

on the controlled persons under the control orders was to deprive them of their liberty; if so, the orders were inconsistent with Article 5. The courts below had held that they were. The House of Lords dismissed the Secretary of State's appeal, although their Lordships were divided: Lord Hoffmann was very clear that the curfew did not involve an unlawful deprivation of liberty.

So now we have TPIMs – Terrorism Prevention and Investigation Measures. These were introduced by the Terrorism Prevention and Investigation Measures Act 2011. By section 1 control orders were abolished. Subject to urgency, the imposition of a TPIM requires the permission of the court (section 6). A TPIM may impose (see Schedule 1) restrictions on residence, travel, movement, association with others, work or studies, and access to finance, property and electronic communication devices. The subject may be required to report to the police, be photographed, and submit to a monitoring device. So far as I know there has not yet been a legal challenge to the use of TPIMs. Indeed, notorious recent instances have given rise to disquiet that they may not be sufficiently effective.

These reflections on the compromise between state security and due process have been directed to measures taken or to be taken against persons in this country whose extremism may put us in danger but who cannot be put on trial. Where the individual is an alien there is a linked but different question: why can he not be peremptorily removed from the United Kingdom? Recent instances will readily come to mind. The government has gritted its teeth and been loyal to the standards of the ECHR.

Conclusions

What does all this tell us about the constitutional balance, and the threat posed by extremism to the moderate liberality of the common law? In the next lecture, 'The Common Law and Europe', I shall suggest that some decisions of our courts on the application of the ECHR have locked the English law of human rights too tightly into the Strasbourg jurisprudence, and for that reason need to be reconsidered. But the recent cases on counter-terrorism legislation, *A and others* and *JJ*, disclose a much more positive dimension of the Human Rights Act. What it has done is to put more teeth in the common law's mouth. It has provided a statutory underpinning for the vindication, to the extent of the remedies which the Act allows, of the common law's founding principles of reason, fairness and the presumption of liberty. In *A and others*, Lord Bingham reported part of the appellants' argument supporting a violation of ECHR Article 5 as follows:

> In urging the fundamental importance of the right to personal freedom ... the appellants were able to draw on the long libertarian tradition of English law, dating back to chapter 39 of Magna Carta 1215, given effect in the ancient remedy of *habeas corpus*, declared in the Petition of Right 1628, upheld in a series of landmark decisions down the centuries and embodied in the substance and procedure of the law to our own day.

I might, I think, be less blithe about the impact of the ECHR on the United Kingdom's ability to remove dangerous extremists from this country.

Finding the right balance between justice and security, deciding how tight should be the knot that ties one hand behind democracy's back, has been painstaking and perhaps painful. I pass no judgement on the wisdom or unwisdom of TPIMs. I have no special claim to know how tight the knot should be. But I think that the dialogue between courts and Parliament faced with the threat of the extremist's agenda has shown the constitutional balance at work. The moderate liberality of the common law has been honed but not subdued by the pressure of security interests; and the pressure, of course, is entirely legitimate. We must be vigilant to see that the pressure is always tested. We must keep the constitutional balance, and in doing so give the principles of the common law – reason, fairness and the presumption of liberty – as big a space as possible.

The defence of the constitutional balance, and of the moderate liberality of the common law, requires that we tolerate the extremist's possession of his doctrine but prevent or punish the execution of his agenda. We need to be clever enough, and brave enough, to face down the difficulties and challenges which that involves. To confront the threats of extremism, more is needed than the muscular provision of TPIMs, control orders or detention. The constitutional balance has to be defended through the precepts of the common law, so that the statutes of Parliament and the policies of government are delivered to the people through the prism of reason, fairness and the presumption of liberty. By this means the legislature is allowed efficacy but forbidden oppression; and our constitution will mark the difference between the extremist's doctrine and his agenda. In considerable measure this is the responsibility of the courts. The judges possess the armoury of their predecessors' wisdom; and they are free of the rancour and asperity of party politics. But they have no tanks to roll onto other people's lawns: as Sir Gerard Brennan, Chief Justice of Australia from 1995 to 1998, said in a lecture at University College Dublin on 22 April 1997,[17] they have 'no power but the power of judgment, [and] no power base but public confidence'. The duty of the judges is to give public confidence to the constitutional balance by the force of their reasoned judgments. If they discharge the duty well, that will play its part in keeping us on the right side of Euthyphro's dilemma. And because the common law is built on the experience of so many conflicting struggles, hopes and fears, it will recall us also to the petition of Aurelius Symmachus to Valentinian II in AD 382:

> We look on the same stars, the heaven is common to us all, the same world surrounds us. What matters it by what arts each of us seeks for truth? We cannot arrive by one and the same path at so great a secret.

[17] 'The Third Branch and the Fourth Estate', second lecture in a series on Broadcasting, Society and the Law, University College Dublin, 22 April 1997.

LECTURE III

The Common Law and Europe

'But when we come to matters with a European element, the Treaty is like an incoming tide. It flows into the estuaries and up the rivers. It cannot be held back. Parliament has decreed that the Treaty is henceforward to be part of our law. It is equal in force to any statute.' This was Lord Denning's metaphor for the arrival in our books of Community law. The citation is from *Bulmer* v. *Bollinger*,[1] a celebrated case at the time. It was about the protection of the designation 'champagne' under what is of course now EU law. Judgment was delivered only sixteen months after the United Kingdom acceded to what was then known as the Common Market in January 1973.

In Lecture I, I described the constitutional balance between law and government, between judicial and political power. The constitutional balance has evolved through the benign force of our constitution's unifying principle, the common law. The common law's distinctive method has yielded a process of continuous self-correction, allowing for the refinement of principle over time; it is the crucible of the moderate and orderly development of state power. This benign continuum of developing law has been the means by which legislature and government are allowed efficacy but forbidden oppression. But I also said that there were two contemporary threats to the constitutional balance. The first

[1] [1974] Ch. 401.

power which the common law provides. But it has its origins in German administrative law from which it was borrowed and thereafter developed by the European Court of Justice.[4] That said, *Schmidt* is perhaps not quite so telling an example of the common law's catholicity. Lord Denning himself has stated that he felt sure that the concept of legitimate expectation 'came out of my own head and not from any continental or other source'.[5] But it has a distinctly European pedigree.

However that may be, the overall point is clear enough: the common law draws inspiration from many sources. Thus, our courts had embarked upon the recognition of fundamental constitutional rights well before the Human Rights Act 1998, and were to no little extent inspired to do so by the yet unincorporated European Convention.[6] Then Lord Diplock in 1984 in the *CCSU* case[7] expressed himself as having in mind 'the possible adoption in the future of the principle of "proportionality" which is recognised in the administrative law of several of our fellow members of the European Economic Community'; since then proportionality has become common currency, and there has

4 The German concept was *Vertrauenschutz*. As for the Luxembourg court, see J. Usher, 'The Influence of National Concepts on Decisions of the European Court' (1976) 1 *European Law Review* 359, 364 and *EC Commission* v. *EC Council* [1973] ECR 575. I owe these references to Prof. B. N. Pandey's article, 'Doctrine of Legitimate Expectation' (2002) 31 *Ban. LJ* 57. See also, among other materials, Prof. C. F. Forsyth [1988] *CLJ* 238.

5 In a letter to Prof. Forsyth, quoted at [1988] *CLJ* 238, 241.

6 See e.g., Murray Hunt, 'The Emergence of a Common Law Human Rights Jurisdiction', ch. 5 in *Using Human Rights Law in English Courts* (Oxford, Hart Publishing, 1997).

7 [1985] AC 374, 410.

been an increasingly lively debate as to whether, or the extent to which, this essentially European concept should be deployed in purely domestic public law cases. So also the idea of legal certainty, articulated as such, has a European parentage and a common law application.

Legitimate expectation, proportionality, legal certainty: our domestic public law, and thus the common law, has been greatly enriched by these European implants. Other examples may no doubt readily be found in other fields, such as the law merchant. We owe our modern understanding of the concept of privacy, which straddles the realms of private and public law alike, very largely to ECHR Article 8; but it has taken root here as an autonomous construct[8] through the medium of the law of confidence. All this, moreover, may be said to march with the common law's take on customary international law. In *Trendtex* v. *Central Bank of Nigeria*[9] in 1976, Lord Denning stated that 'the rules of international law are incorporated into English law automatically'.

This, then, is the catholicity of the common law. It was Rudyard Kipling who coined the phrase, '[w]hat should they know of England, who only England know?'.[10] Our law has embraced these legal importations from foreign sources as its own. They have become part of the means of the common law's power of continuous self-correction. They go in the scales of the constitutional balance; they have refined it and lent it nuance. In making them our own we

[8] See in particular the judgment of Sedley LJ in *Douglas and another* v. *Hello! Ltd* [2001] QB 967.

[9] [1977] 1 QB 529. [10] Rudyard Kipling, *The English Flag* (1891).

have refashioned them, or some of them, to bear the colour and stamp of common law principle. Thus in *SS (Nigeria)*[11] in May 2013, I said:

> There is no doubt that proportionality imposes a more demanding standard of public decision-making than conventional *Wednesbury* review, whose essence is simply an appeal to the rule of reason. But the true innovation effected by proportionality is not . . . to be defined in terms of judicial intrusion or activism. Rather it consists in the introduction into judicial review and like forms of process of a principle which might be a child of the common law itself: it may be (and often has been) called the principle of minimal interference. It is that every intrusion by the State upon the freedom of the individual stands in need of justification. Accordingly, any interference which is greater than required for the State's proper purpose cannot be justified. This is at the core of proportionality; it articulates the discipline which proportionality imposes on decision-makers.[12]

What is the threat to this catholicity of the common law? It starts from the fact that these principles with a foreign ancestry, like any other principle of the common law, can only truly take their place and play their part if the law's users, its practitioners and its commentators, believe in their benign effects. In the end the law's authority rests upon public belief. In Lecture II, I cited Sir Gerard Brennan, Chief Justice of Australia from 1995 to 1998, who said in a lecture at University

[11] [2013] EWCA Civ 550. [12] *Ibid.* para. 38.

College Dublin in 1997[13] that the common law courts have 'no power but the power of judgment, [and] no power base but public confidence'.

Now, I have come to think that the political controversies and resentments concerning Europe, in which of course I have no voice and claim none, may undermine the confidence which thinking people ought to have in the common law's catholicity: in its use of principles which were born or have flourished in Luxembourg and in Strasbourg. The threat takes different forms as between the two. As for Luxembourg, it is intertwined with fears of the loss, or at least the erosion, of state sovereignty. As for Strasbourg, it is intertwined with a resentment felt among many shades of opinion that under the pressure of the Strasbourg court the law of human rights has got too big. These are the incoming tides, to use Lord Denning's metaphor, which it is feared cannot be held back. The threat to the common law is that these fears may undermine the confidence which ought to be reposed in the common law's enrichment by our legal importations from Europe. It is therefore of the first importance that interested parties – lawyers and others – should have the imagination and discernment to see that the common law's catholicity, its ingenious deployment of sources from outside itself, has a value of its own, entirely unconnected with the politics of Europe or the tide of human rights. And upon this a further perception follows. When they cross the Channel, these principles and ideas are absorbed into the common law's

13 'The Third Branch and the Fourth Estate', second lecture in a series on Broadcasting, Society and the Law, University College Dublin, 22 April 1997.

autonomy; that is, their development in this jurisdiction is in the hands of our judges, as surely as the duty of care in negligence or the doctrine of consideration in the law of contract.

These are the general truths I would emphasise. But there are more specific antidotes for the fears and resentments which seem to be fuelled by Luxembourg (or Brussels) and Strasbourg. My prescription for the first – Luxembourg – is a correct understanding of the European Union's position in the constitution of the United Kingdom. My remedy for the second – Strasbourg – is to revisit our domestic case law concerning the interpretation and application of the Human Rights Act. Let me turn to state sovereignty and the European Union.

State Sovereignty and the European Union

State sovereignty is the legal autonomy of the nation state, given and guaranteed by the state's own law. I leave aside questions of the diplomatic recognition by others of the state's sovereignty. At the present time, the British state enjoys this legal autonomy. It has not been ceded to any other entity; it has not been ceded to the European Union. Neither the European Communities Act 1972, which of course took us into the Community, nor any other statute touching our membership of the Union, has done so or purported to do so. Indeed, as a matter of constitutional theory, no Act of Parliament is capable of ceding altogether the sovereignty of the state. An Act of Parliament can be repealed; so long as there is a power to repeal any Act which purports to cede sovereignty, of necessity sovereignty remains, so to speak, at home; it inheres in the very power of repeal, which contradicts sovereignty's transfer elsewhere. The cession of state sovereignty would therefore require a shift in what is recognised as law; a change in what Prof. H. L. A. Hart called the 'rule of recognition'.[14] The new rule would have to confirm the efficacy of a law that could not be repealed. Since the cession of state sovereignty, were such a thing ever to be contemplated, would no doubt be fraught with acute and bitter controversy, the conditions of general acceptance which a new rule of recognition requires would not readily be met.

But this is theoretical, far distant from the real world. These matters are, however, worth noting, because they represent a fundamental legal truth concerning state sovereignty in the United Kingdom: strictly speaking, it cannot be ceded by law without the recognition of a new kind of statute. Of course a *de facto* cession of sovereignty might come to be treated as *de jure* with the passage of time, and there are instances of statutes which could not in practice be repealed, such as the Statute of Westminster 1931. There are also cases where the validity of a statute seems indeed to be based upon a new rule of recognition, such as the Parliament Act 1911. But all these are even further distant from my subject in this Lecture. The fears and resentments relating to the European Union which threaten the common law's catholicity are not of anything so outlandish as a cession of state sovereignty, despite the language in which they are sometimes expressed. Rather,

[14] H. L. A. Hart, *The Concept of Law* (Oxford, Clarendon Press, 1961; Penelope Bulloch and Joseph Raz (eds.), 2nd edn, 1994), published after Hart's death.

they concern the extent of the limited powers that have in fact been transferred to the Union and may be so transferred in the future.

However, this rather more practical concern also raises constitutional questions. There is one case in which the Divisional Court was asked to confront the legal relationship between the powers of Westminster and the powers of Brussels, *Thoburn* v. *Sunderland City Council*[15] in 2002. I must therefore try your patience with citations from my judgment in that case, with which Crane J agreed. I hope you will not think it too reminiscent of that caustic line in the movie *Two for the Road*,[16] about taking the salute at an endless march past of oneself.

Thoburn v. *Sunderland City Council*

Thoburn (the so-called 'Metric Martyrs' case) was directly concerned with the doctrine of implied repeal. It was contended that section 1 of the Weights and Measures Act 1985 effected an implied repeal of section 2(2) of the European Communities Act 1972 'to the extent that the latter empowered the making of any provision by way of subordinate legislation . . . which would be inconsistent with that section'.[17]

I need not take time with the details of the argument, or the complex web of subordinate legislation that was involved. The submission on implied repeal failed for various reasons. What matters for present purposes is the court's

[15] [2003] QB 151. [16] With Albert Finney and Audrey Hepburn.
[17] *Thoburn* [2003] QB 151, para. 39.

response to an argument advanced for the respondent (by Eleanor Sharpston QC, now the British Advocate General at the Court of Justice of the European Union) which 'proceeded on the assumption that the incorporation of EU law effected by the [European Communities Act] ... must have included not only the whole corpus of European law upon substantive matters such as ... the free movement of goods ... but also any jurisprudence of the Court of Justice, or other rule of Community law, which purports to touch the constitutional preconditions upon which the sovereign legislative power belonging to a member State may be exercised'.[18] Anticipating, as it were, what I have said in this Lecture about the rule of recognition, I responded thus:

> Whatever may be the position elsewhere, the law of England disallows any such assumption. Parliament cannot bind its successors by stipulating against repeal, wholly or partly, of the ECA. It cannot stipulate as to the manner and form of any subsequent legislation ... Thus there is nothing in the ECA which allows the Court of Justice, or any other institutions of the EU, to touch or qualify the conditions of Parliament's legislative supremacy in the United Kingdom. Not because the legislature chose not to allow it; because by our law it could not allow it. That being so, the legislative and judicial institutions of the EU cannot intrude upon those conditions. The British Parliament has not the authority to authorise any such thing. Being sovereign, it cannot abandon its sovereignty ... This is, of course, the traditional doctrine of sovereignty. If it is to be

[18] *Ibid.* para. 58.

> modified, it certainly cannot be done by the incorporation of external texts. The conditions of Parliament's legislative supremacy in the United Kingdom necessarily remain in the United Kingdom's hands. But the traditional doctrine has in my judgment been modified. It has been done by the common law, wholly consistently with constitutional principle.[19]

The modification there referred to was the proposed acknowledgement of a category of statutes which may be called 'constitutional' statutes,[20] which include the European Communities Act. Other examples are the Magna Carta, the Bill of Rights 1689, the Act of Union, the Reform Acts which distributed and enlarged the franchise, the Human Rights Act 1998, the Scotland Act 1998 and the Government of Wales Act 1998:

> Ordinary statutes may be impliedly repealed. Constitutional statutes may not. For the repeal of a constitutional Act or the abrogation of a fundamental right to be effected by statute, the court would apply this test: is it shown that the legislature's *actual* – not imputed, constructive or presumed – intention was to effect the repeal or abrogation? . . . The ordinary rule of implied repeal . . . has no application to constitutional statutes.[21]

[19] *Ibid.* para. 59.

[20] There is a valuable discussion of this idea, including important criticisms of my approach in *Thoburn*, by Prof. David Feldman, 'The Nature and Significance of "Constitutional" Legislation' (2013) 129 *LQR* 343.

[21] *Thoburn* [2003] QB 151, para. 63.

This acknowledgement of the European Communities Act 1972 as a constitutional statute sought to reconcile Parliament's power of repeal with the result of the House of Lords' decision in *Factortame (No. 1)*.[22] In that case the House was faced with a statute, the Merchant Shipping Act 1988, which included provisions in breach of EU rights and which (it might be thought) was to that extent inconsistent with the European Communities Act 1972. On conventional doctrine, the Merchant Shipping Act would by implication have repealed the European Communities Act *pro tanto*. But such an outcome was not even argued in *Factortame*. Sir William Wade regarded the result in that case as 'revolutionary',[23] for it appeared from Lord Bridge's reasoning that Parliament by the Act of 1972 had succeeded in binding its successors. On the approach taken in *Thoburn*, however, it has done nothing of the kind; *Thoburn* shows that the Act of 1972 could only be repealed by express provision, which the Merchant Shipping Act certainly did not purport to do.

The point for present purposes is that the levers of constitutional power are in law untouched by our membership of the European Union. '[T]he courts have found their way through the *impasse* seemingly created by two supremacies, the supremacy of European law and the supremacy of Parliament';[24] and the supremacy which European law possesses in this jurisdiction is entirely given by the United

[22] [1990] 2 AC 85.

[23] H. W. R. Wade and C. F. Forsyth, *Administrative Law* (Oxford, Clarendon Press, 2000).

[24] *Thoburn* [2003] QB 151, para. 60.

Kingdom Parliament. To that extent European measures, so far as they are effective in this jurisdiction, possess a principal characteristic of secondary legislation: they only have force to the extent permitted by the enabling Act. Now, it is well established by the common law that secondary legislation cannot lawfully abrogate a fundamental or constitutional right unless the enabling statute gives authority for that to be done by express words or the clearest implication.[25] But section 2 of the European Communities Act is expressed in very general terms. In *Thoburn*, I said:

> In the event, which no doubt would never happen in the real world, that a European measure was seen to be repugnant to a fundamental or constitutional right guaranteed by the law of England, a question would arise whether the general words of the ECA were sufficient to incorporate the measure and give it overriding effect in domestic law.[26]

And so, because the supremacy which European law possesses in this jurisdiction is given by the United Kingdom Parliament, the reach of European law is ultimately a function of Parliament's will; and it is, of course, not to be assumed that Parliament has given the European legislature *carte blanche*.

I hope it goes without saying that this conspectus of the edge of power between Brussels and Westminster implies no hostility to anything European. I would have no business peddling such an opinion, even if I harboured it. I have been

[25] See e.g., *Ex parte Witham* [1998] 2 WLR 849; *Ex parte Pierson* [1998] AC 539, 575C–D; *Ex parte Simms* [2000] 2 AC 115.

[26] *Thoburn* [2003] QB 151, para. 69.

concerned only to describe what in law is the constitutional position as I see it. And the constitutional position thus described is in truth ring-fenced from the storms of controversy over the content of EU law. The development of our public law, enriched as I have said by ideas that come from Europe, should be no less secure. The common law's catholicity – its absorption of principles such as proportionality – has nothing at all to do with the politics of Europe. That is how they should be seen and understood. Indeed, there is every reason to suppose, and for my part I hope, that even if the United Kingdom were to secede from the Union, these principles would continue to mature within the fabric of the common law, and enrich the constitutional balance.

Strasbourg

Now I will move from Brussels and Luxembourg to Strasbourg. As I said at the start, the common law's catholicity is threatened not only by the perceived effects of EU law, but also those of the law of human rights. However, the perceived effects of human rights law also threatens another virtue of the common law: its restraint. The charge is that the law of human rights has got too big. It has pushed the judges into the field of political decisions. Here the threat to the law's catholicity and to its restraint march together. To the extent that the law is or seems to be driven by decisions of the Strasbourg court, we are looking again at Lord Denning's unstoppable tide, flowing up the estuaries and the rivers; or at least, the perception of it. Just as with the European Union, the resulting fears and resentments may undermine the confidence which thinking people ought to have in the common law's catholicity, for our common law principles with a European source, most notably proportionality, have their parentage in Strasbourg as well as Luxembourg. But if we can make the law of human rights truly our own, perceived and rightly perceived as a construct of English law, we shall quell these fears of the incoming tide and so protect the common law's catholicity, and at the same time keep control of the proper place of human rights, and so protect the common law's restraint.

Are our courts more subservient than they need be to the jurisprudence of the European Court of Human Rights? Have they fettered their historic autonomy and undercut their own power of judgment – the very power that enables them to keep the constitutional balance? This is not, I must confess, by any means a new debate. There have been eloquent calls for looser ties between our courts and Strasbourg for some time. Lord Irvine of Lairg and Jack Straw MP, who sponsored the Human Rights Bill in the Lords and Commons respectively, have been muscular advocates for such an outcome – Jack Straw in the second of his Hamlyn Lectures, delivered in 2012.[27] So has Baroness Hale, speaking extra-judicially.[28] And

[27] Jack Straw, 'The Human Rights Act and Europe', ch. 2 in *Aspects of Law Reform: An Insider's Perspective, Hamlyn Lectures 2012* (Cambridge University Press, 2013). Lord Irvine gave a lecture entitled 'A British Interpretation of Convention Rights', UCL Judicial Institute, 14 December 2011. Sir Philip Sales published a reply: 'Strasbourg Jurisprudence and the Human Rights Act: A Response to Lord Irvine' (2012) *PL* 253.

[28] '*Argentoratum Locutum*: Is the Supreme Court Supreme?', Nottingham Human Rights Lecture 2011, 1 December 2011.

Lord Reed, in a lecture at the Inner Temple earlier this month,[29] has expounded and emphasised the primacy of the common law's protection of human rights. I travel this ground again because I think there remain important questions as to the relationship between the Human Rights Act 1998 and the Convention jurisprudence which touch the catholicity and the restraint of the common law, and because there have been some very recent important developments in the Supreme Court, including one case (*Osborn*) referred to by Lord Reed in his lecture and in which he gave the first judgment.

If statute required such subservience of our courts to Strasbourg as to fetter their historic autonomy and undercut their power of judgment, then the legislature would itself have assaulted the constitutional balance. We must start with section 2(1) of the Human Rights Act 1998:

> A court or tribunal determining a question which has arisen in connection with a Convention right must take into account any –
> (a) judgment, decision, declaration or advisory opinion of the European Court of Human Rights,
> (b) opinion of the Commission . . . ,
> (c) decision of the Commission . . . , or
> (d) decision of the Committee of Ministers . . .
> whenever made or given, so far as, in the opinion of the court or tribunal, it is relevant to the proceedings in which that question has arisen.

[29] Lord Reed, 'The Common Law and the ECHR'.

Ullah

How have the courts discharged their duty under section 2? The case of *Ullah* in June 2004[30] concerned the right to freedom of thought, conscience and religion guaranteed by Article 9 of the Convention. Lord Bingham said this:

> [T]he House is required by section 2(1) of the Human Rights Act 1998 to take into account any relevant Strasbourg case law. While such case law is not strictly binding, it has been held that courts should, in the absence of some special circumstances, follow any clear and constant jurisprudence of the Strasbourg court: *R (Alconbury Developments Ltd)* v. *Secretary of State for the Environment, Transport and the Regions* [2001] UKHL 23, [2003] 2 AC 295, paragraph 26. This reflects the fact that the Convention is an international instrument, the correct interpretation of which can be authoritatively expounded only by the Strasbourg court. From this it follows that a national court subject to a duty such as that imposed by section 2 should not without strong reason dilute or weaken the effect of the Strasbourg case law. It is indeed unlawful under section 6 of the 1998 Act for a public authority, including a court, to act in a way which is incompatible with a Convention right. It is of course open to member states to provide for rights more generous than those guaranteed by the Convention, but such provision should not be the product of interpretation of the Convention by national courts, since the meaning of the Convention should be uniform throughout the states party to it. The duty of

30 [2004] 2 AC 323.

> national courts is to keep pace with the Strasbourg jurisprudence as it evolves over time: no more, but certainly no less.[31]

This statement of high authority has been repeatedly followed since. The last sentence – '[t]he duty of national courts is to keep pace with the Strasbourg jurisprudence' – has been taken to indicate that the Strasbourg cases should generally, even if not rigidly, be treated as authoritative: as having the effect of legal precedent, or something very close to it. With deference to the House of Lords, and with great respect for Lord Bingham, I have in common with others come to think that this approach represents an important wrong turning in our law. I will come to the reasons more fully. Essentially (1) section 2 of the 1998 Act enjoins no subservience to the Strasbourg jurisprudence – it is to be '[taken] into account'. (2) Lord Bingham's reference to 'the correct interpretation' of the Convention, and his statement that it is in the hands of the Strasbourg court, implies that there is such a thing: a single correct interpretation, a universal jurisprudence, across the boundaries of the signatory states. I think that is a mistake. (3) So close an adherence to Strasbourg gravely undermines the autonomous development of human rights law by the common law courts. As I have said: unless we make the law of human rights truly our own, we shall not quell the fears of Lord Denning's tide, and we shall put at risk the catholicity and the restraint of the common law.

There has, it is true, been some slippage from the unqualified *Ullah* position. Lord Phillips in a 2010

[31] *Ibid.* para. 20. Cf. Lord Brown in *Al-Skeini* [2007] UKHL 26.

case[32] referred to 'rare occasions where the domestic court has concerns as to whether a decision of the Strasbourg court sufficiently appreciates or accommodates particular aspects of our domestic process. In such circumstances it is open to the domestic court to decline to follow the Strasbourg decision'.[33] Lord Neuberger has stated that '[t]his court is not bound to follow every decision of the European court. Not only would it be impractical to do so: it would sometimes be inappropriate, as it would destroy the ability of the court to engage in the constructive dialogue with the European court which is of value to the development of Convention law'.[34] But the *Ullah* doctrine has not been overturned.

Osborn

The latest word is to be found in two very recent decisions of the Supreme Court, *Osborn*[35] and *Chester*,[36] in each of which judgment was delivered in October 2013. In *Osborn*, Lord Reed emphasised that:

> [t]he values underlying both the Convention and our own constitution require that Convention rights should be protected primarily by a detailed body of domestic law. The Convention taken by itself is too inspecific to provide the guidance which is necessary in a state governed by the rule of law ... The importance of the [Human Rights] Act is unquestionable. It does not however supersede the

[32] *R* v. *Horncastle* [2010] 2 AC 373. [33] *Ibid.* para. 11.
[34] *Manchester City Council* v. *Pinnock* [2011] 2 AC 104, para. 48.
[35] [2013] UKSC 61. [36] [2013] UKSC 63.

> protection of human rights under the common law or statute, or create a discrete body of law based upon the judgments of the European court. Human rights continue to be protected by our domestic law, interpreted and developed in accordance with the Act when appropriate.[37]

This emphasis on the primary protections offered by the common law is, with respect, very important and surely to be welcomed. This reasoning shows that it should often be unnecessary to have recourse to the Convention. But it does not tell us how to interpret the Convention where the case in hand requires that to be done; and there may be a question (as Lord Reed acknowledged[38]) – indeed there very often is – whether compliance with the common law will satisfy the Convention. More radically, there are some cases where the common law has no or virtually no free-standing voice because the human rights issue arises out of a statutory provision or provisions which are wholly unambiguous. That is so in relation to prisoners' voting rights, with which the other Supreme Court case from last month, *Chester*, was concerned.

Chester

In *Chester*, the Attorney General invited the Supreme Court not to apply the principles in the two Strasbourg decisions, *Hirst* v. *United Kingdom (No. 2)*[39] and *Scoppola* v. *Italy (No. 3)*,[40] which dealt with prisoners' voting rights. The court declined the invitation. Lord Mance referred to the views of

[37] *Osborn* [2013] UKSC 61, paras. 56–7. [38] *Ibid.* para. 101.
[39] (2005) 42 EHRR 41. [40] (2013) 56 EHRR 19.

Lord Phillips and Lord Neuberger which I have cited. Then he stated:[41]

> It would have then to involve some truly fundamental principle of our law or some most egregious oversight or misunderstanding before it could be appropriate for this Court to contemplate an outright refusal to follow Strasbourg authority at the Grand Chamber level.

Lord Sumption referred[42] to the 'international obligation of the United Kingdom under Article 46.1 of the Convention to abide by the decisions of the European Court of Human Rights in any case to which it is a party', and noted[43] that this obligation 'goes further than section 2(1) of the Act, but it is not one of the provisions to which the [Human Rights] Act gives effect'. Then this:

> In the ordinary use of language, to 'take into account' a decision of the European Court of Human Rights means no more than to consider it, which is consistent with rejecting it as wrong. However, this is not an approach that a United Kingdom court can adopt, save in altogether exceptional cases. The courts have for many years interpreted statutes and developed the common law so as to achieve consistency between the domestic law of the United Kingdom and its international obligations, so far as they are free to do so. In enacting the Human Rights Act 1998, Parliament must be taken to have been aware that effect would be given to the Act in accordance with this long-standing principle. A decision of the European Court of Human Rights is more than an opinion about the meaning of the

[41] *Chester* [2013] UKSC 63, para. 27. [42] *Ibid.* para. 119. [43] *Ibid.* para. 120.

> Convention. It is an adjudication by the tribunal which the United Kingdom has by treaty agreed should give definitive rulings on the subject. The courts are therefore bound to treat them as the authoritative expositions of the Convention which the Convention intends them to be, unless it is apparent that it has misunderstood or overlooked some significant feature of English law or practice which may, when properly explained, lead to the decision being reviewed by the Strasbourg Court.

A Different Approach?

I cannot do justice in the course of this Lecture to all the learning on the relation between our courts and Strasbourg, or even to the fullness of the *Osborn* and *Chester* decisions. But perhaps I may pick out two statements from our highest court which seem to me to be at the core of the matter. Lord Bingham in *Ullah*: 'the correct interpretation of [the Convention] can be authoritatively expounded only by the Strasbourg court ... the meaning of the Convention should be uniform throughout the states party to it'. Lord Sumption in *Chester*: 'a decision of the European Court of Human Rights ... is an adjudication by the tribunal which the United Kingdom has by treaty agreed should give definitive rulings on the subject. The courts are therefore bound to treat them as the authoritative expositions of the Convention'.

So the House of Lords and the Supreme Court have accorded overriding force to the notion that only Strasbourg's rulings on the Convention are 'definitive' or 'authoritative'. Why should this be so? Section 2 of the Human Rights Act 1998 cannot surely bear such a weight. The expression 'take into account' simply does not mean 'follow' or 'treat as binding' (or something close to it). But the point on the interpretation of section 2(1) is stronger than this. As Jack Straw points out,[44] decisions of the Commission and Council of Ministers are to be taken into account under section 2(1) no less than judgments of the court; and decisions of the Council, at least, are 'wholly political'. Parliament surely cannot have intended, by deployment of the phrase 'take into account', that our courts should treat such decisions as effectively determining the jurisprudence of the Convention for the purposes of its application in the United Kingdom. Yet the term 'take into account' must mean the same across all its applications in the subsection.

Perhaps the reason for this deference to the Strasbourg court, apparently quite unwarranted by the statute, lies in Lord Sumption's reference to the United Kingdom's obligations under Article 46.1 of the Convention. That provides:

> The High Contracting Parties undertake to abide by the final judgement of the Court in any case to which they are parties.

So the United Kingdom must fulfil rulings of the Strasbourg court in cases brought against it. But this is an obligation which sounds in public international law; it forms no part whatever of our domestic law. As Lord Sumption pointed out, Article 46.1 has not been incorporated by the Human Rights Act 1998. Unlike, for example, France and Germany, we do not have a

[44] Straw, *Aspects of Law Reform: An Insider's Perspective*, n. 27 above, p. 31.

monist constitution by which a treaty, once entered into, automatically becomes part of the state's own law. Under our dualist constitution, international treaties are entered into by the executive government; and the executive is not generally a source of law in England. And Article 46, moreover, of course, says nothing whatever about how a signatory state is to treat Strasbourg cases to which it has not been a party.

There is, with respect, no reason that I can see to conclude that the obligation of Article 46.1 offers any aid to the true interpretation of section 2(1) of the Human Rights Act 1998. Lord Sumption refers to the long-standing practice of our courts to interpret statutes so as to achieve consistency between the domestic law of the United Kingdom and its international obligations.[45] But the development of a domestic law of human rights, taking account (in the proper but limited sense of the term) of the Strasbourg cases, offers no affront whatever to Article 46.1 or any other international obligation. Article 46.1 means only that once a case involving the United Kingdom has been decided in Strasbourg, the United Kingdom must abide by the result. That is a very far distance from the notion that, for example, Strasbourg judgments on Article 8, which on the facts may have nothing whatever to do with the United Kingdom, are authoritative for the purpose of the Human Rights Act.

If neither section 2 of the Act, nor Article 46 of the Convention, justifies the judicial deference under which we have laboured since the *Ullah* case, what remains? A distinctive human rights jurisprudence of our own must, of

[45] See e.g., *Garland* v. *British Rail Engineering* [1983] 2 AC 751.

course, acknowledge that Strasbourg may take a different view of the same case; and Article 46 would then bite and the United Kingdom would be obliged to give effect to the Strasbourg decision. But I cannot see that our courts should be discouraged by that possibility. As I have said, Lord Neuberger referred to 'the ability of the court to engage in the constructive dialogue with the European court which is of value to the development of Convention law'. That ability, and that value, may be increased, not diminished, by our own initiatives in the field. We should have the confidence to act on that premise.

The constructive dialogue of which Lord Neuberger spoke, if we pursue it vigorously, may enrich not only the development of Convention law, but will also allow our own constitutional law to flourish. By our constitution, there is an important difference between the protection of fundamental values and the formulation of state policy: broadly, the former is the business of the courts and the latter the business of elected government. The greatest challenge of our human rights law is that it appears to merge these two ideas. Not least in the litigation of claims for the protection of private or family life under ECHR Article 8 we encounter muscular disputes as to whether the government measure in question, perhaps a deportation decision, is properly within the sphere of policy or is an unwarranted intrusion upon the individual's rights. In such a case, the debate is not only about the weight to be accorded to the Convention right on the merits. It is about the respective roles of government and judiciary. In this jurisdiction, despite the brickbats daily thrown at politicians, there remains a deep sense that matters of state policy are in essence the responsibility of the elected arms of government. But in other states, no less democratic than our own, a different view may be taken of the respective roles of the judicial and the elected arms of state power. Constitutional conditions – including the actual and perceived authority of legislature, executive and judiciary – differ from state to state, and cultural and historic factors may feed the differences.

The historic role of the law of human rights is the protection of what are properly regarded as fundamental values. It is not to make marginal choices about issues upon which reasonable, humane and informed people may readily disagree. I acknowledge that the boundary between proper policy and the vindication of rights is difficult. What is a policy issue to one man's mind is a human rights issue to another. Certainly, there will come a point – and it is a very important point – where the law of human rights must be allowed to say, 'Thus far but no further'. Fundamental values possess at the very least an irreducible minimum. Torture, the suppression of free speech or disregard of due process are not matters of legitimate disagreement, but of shame. However, in a debate on Convention issues where there may be more than one civilised view, the balance to be struck between policy and rights, between the judiciary and government, is surely a matter for national constitutions. This is why, with very great respect, I would venture to question Lord Bingham's statement in *Ullah* that 'the correct interpretation of [the Convention] can be authoritatively expounded only by the Strasbourg court ... the meaning of the Convention should be uniform throughout the states party to it'. There may perfectly properly be different answers to some human rights issues in different states on similar facts. I think the Strasbourg court should recognise this. The means of doing so is readily at hand: the doctrine of the margin of appreciation. As Lord Reed said in his lecture at the Inner Temple, 'in the Convention case law the principle of proportionality is indissolubly linked to the concept of the margin of appreciation'.

There is a recent sign that our courts may be becoming readier to spread their wings. In *AG's Reference No. 96 of 2013*,[46] in which judgment was delivered on 18 February 2014, the Criminal Division of the Court of Appeal had to address the reasoning of the Grand Chamber of the European Court of Human Rights in *Vinter*,[47] which concerned provisions of United Kingdom law relevant to the imposition of whole life prison terms. The Strasbourg court had regard to the Secretary of State's power under section 30 of the Crime (Sentences) Act 1997 to 'release a life prisoner on licence if he is satisfied that exceptional circumstances exist which justify the prisoner's release on compassionate grounds'. In the *AG's Reference* case at paragraph 28, the Lord Chief Justice summarised the Strasbourg court's reasoning:

> The Grand Chamber therefore concluded that s.30 did not, because of the lack of certainty, provide an appropriate and adequate avenue of redress in the event an offender sought to show that his continued imprisonment was not justified.

Paragraph 129 of the Strasbourg judgment is then cited, setting out the court's reasoning. The Lord Chief Justice concluded:

[46] [2014] EWCA Crim 188. [47] Applications 66069/09, 130/10 and 3896/10.

> We disagree. In our view, the domestic law of England and Wales is clear as to 'possible exceptional release of whole life prisoners'.

Conclusion

The Strasbourg case law is not part of the law of England; the Human Rights Convention is. The Convention can be and should be a great force for good in this jurisdiction; as I said in Lecture II, it puts more teeth in the common law's mouth. If we develop it according to the methods and principles of the common law, it will enrich us. Any threat to the common law's catholicity will be dissipated. As for the common law's restraint, we are entitled to think that human rights are like the human heart: the bigger they get, the weaker they get.

In these Lectures I have been concerned with the constitutional balance between law and government. It is harboured and matured by the common law's process of continuous self-correction, which allows the refinement of principle over time, and therefore the orderly development of state power. As I said in Lecture I, the challenge in the end is simply expressed: it is to keep the constitutional balance, and thus to give the principles of the common law – reason, fairness and the presumption of liberty – as big a space as possible. It is no easy challenge. Because our law is constantly renewed by the force of fresh examples; because it reflects and moderates the temper of the people as age succeeds age; because it builds on the experience of ordinary struggles, its principles will always be buffeted by events. In their different ways the confrontation of extremism, and the absorption of law from Europe (the subject of these last two Lectures), press upon the constitutional balance. But if we keep faith with it, we shall enjoy a noble inheritance, and may anticipate a tranquil future.

INDEX

absolutism, 17, 29, 34–6
Act of Union, 5, 68
Allan, Trevor, 27
authority, 10, 17, 25, 41, 43, 67–70

balance, xv–4, 8, 24, 30, 51, 55, 83
belief systems, 33–6
beliefs, 34, 41, 43–8, 62
believers, 32–4, 40, 48
benign continuum of developing law, 3, 18, 57
Bill of Rights, 5, 68
Bingham, Lord, 74–5, 79
black-letter law, 21–3
Blackstone, 11–12
Bonham's case, 11–12
Brussels; *see also* European Union, 6, 64–6, 70–1
Bulmer v Bollinger, 57
Burke, Edmund, 8

catholicity, 4, 29, 58–64, 71–5, 85
cession of state sovereignty, 65
Chester case, 76–9
Coke, Sir Edward, 11–12, 22, 44
compromise, xv, 24–31, 34, 51–3
confidence, 34, 56, 61–3, 71, 82
conscience, 17, 44, 74
constitutional balance, 4, 14, 18–25, 26, 29, 30, 31, 32, 46–51, 54–7, 61, 71–3, 85–6
constitutional powers, 50, 69
constitutional statutes, 68–9
construction; *see also* interpretation, 6, 21–4
constructive dialogue, 76, 82
continuous self-correction, xiii, 9, 12, 16, 57, 61, 85
control orders, 49, 52–3
Convention law/rights, *see* European Convention on Human Rights.
correct interpretation, 74–5, 79, 83
customary international law, 61

deference, 75, 80–1
democracy, 27, 34, 51–5
Denning, Lord, 57–63, 71, 75
detention without trial, 49, 52
dialogue, 27, 34, 55
  constructive, 76, 82
Dicey, 12
discretion, 9, 24
discrimination, 47, 52
distinctive method, 3, 6–10, 30, 57
domestic law, 12, 61, 70, 76–81, 85
due process, 32, 48–53, 83
duties, 5–6, 18, 36, 46–50, 56, 64, 74

efficacy, 3, 18, 24, 29–31, 55–7, 65
elaboration of principle, 18, 23–4, 31

Europe, vi, xiv–4, 9, 25, 29, 54, 84–6
politics of, 63, 71
and sovereignty, 64–6
European Communities Act, 5–6, 64–70
European Convention on Human Rights, xiv, 12–13, 44, 54–8, 60–4, 84–5
European Court of Human Rights, xiv, 54–8, 63–4, 84–5
European Court of Justice, 60, 67
European Union, 12–13, 58, 64–71
Euthyphro's dilemma, xiii, 34–7, 39–42, 56
right arm of, 35, 38, 42, 47
wrong arm of, 35–7, 39–42
expectations, legitimate, xiv, 59–61
extremism, xiii–4, 31–56, 86
nature of, 32–4

fairness, 3, 7, 16, 22–31, 38, 43, 46–8, 54–5, 85
faith, 33, 37–9, 47, 86
fears, xiv, 46–8, 56, 63–5, 71–2, 75
forbidden oppression, 3, 24, 29–31, 55–7
fourfold method, xiii, 7, 20–8
free speech, 10, 47–8, 83
freedom, 5, 12, 28, 34, 39, 44–5, 54, 62, 74
harmony of freedom and justice, 30–1
Freeman, Charles, 37
fundamental rights, 12–13, 21, 28

Gibbon, 9–10
God, 35, 37–40
Goldsworthy, Jeffrey, 17, 28
good faith, 16
Government of Wales Act, 68
government policy, 3, 24, 31, 59
grammar, 21–4, 31

harmony of freedom and justice, 30–1
Hart, HLA, 65
Hooker, Richard, 40
human rights; *see also* European Convention on Human Rights, xii–iv, 6, 12–14, 25, 44, 52–63, 84–5
Human Rights Act, 6, 12–14, 52–4, 58–64, 68, 73–4, 78–81
Hume's Law, 36

imagination, 30, 35, 63
immediacy of political will, 24, 29–31
implied repeal, 66–8
incitement to crime, 45–8
intentions, 13, 68
international obligations, 78–81
interpretation, 3, 20–31, 64, 74, 80–1
see also construction.
correct, 74–5, 79, 83
interpreters, 3, 19–20

judges, 6, 9–11, 17–20, 22–8, 49, 56, 64, 71
judgment, power of, 56, 63, 72–3
judicial review, 3, 14–18, 23–7, 62
jurisdiction, 3, 10, 14–17, 25
judiciary, 22–3, 82–3
jurisprudence, 14, 59, 67, 72, 80
universal, 75
Justinian, 9

Latham, RTE, 4
Laws of Ecclesiastical Polity, The, 40

legal validity, 17
legislative powers, 10, 67
legislative sovereignty, 12, 26, 29
legislative supremacy, 14, 27–8, 67–8
legislature, 3, 11, 16–21, 23–4, 28–32, 55–7, 67–8, 73, 83
legitimate expectations, xiv, 59–61
Lewis, Bernard, 38
liberty, 11, 27, 39, 47–9, 52–3
  see also freedom.
  presumption of, 3, 7, 22–31, 43, 46–50, 54–5, 85
life prisoners, 84–5
Locke, John, 41

Magna Carta, 5, 54, 68
McGarry, John, 28
Merchant Shipping Act, 69
moderate liberality of the common law, 4, 29, 31–2, 42, 46–51, 54–5
morals, 17, 36

naturalistic fallacy, 36
Neuberger, Lord, 76–7, 82

oppression, 3, 18
  forbidden, 3, 24, 29–31, 55–7
orderly development of state power, 9, 29, 57, 85
ordinary struggles, experience of, xv, 7, 29, 32, 43, 85
Osborn case, 73, 76–7

Parliamentary sovereignty, 3–4, 11–14, 18, 23–8
personal freedom, 54
Plato, xiii, 17–19, 34
political extremism, *see* extremism.
political will, immediacy of, 24, 29–31
powers, 5–6, 15–16, 23–6, 50–1, 66
  constitutional, 50, 69
  of judgment, 56, 63, 72–3
  legislative, 10, 67
  state, *see* state power.
  statutory, 23–5
precedent, 7–8, 44, 75
prerogative writs, 14–16
presumption of liberty, 3, 7, 22–31, 43, 46–50, 54–5, 85
privacy, 10, 61
proportionality, xiv, 50, 60–2, 71–2, 84
public bodies, 16, 20, 25, 59
Puritan principle, 41

reasonableness, 16, 41
recognition, rule of, 65–7
Reed, Lord, 72–3, 77, 84
Reform Acts, 68
religion, 37–42, 44–5, 74
repeal, 64–5, 67–9
  implied, 66–8
restraint, 4, 25, 29, 49, 58, 71–5, 85
retrospectivity, presumption against, 21
review, judicial, *see* judicial review.
right arm of Euthyphro's dilemma, 35, 38, 42, 47
rights, 5, 27–8, 48, 68, 74, 83
  Convention, 13, 76
  human, *see* human rights.
  procedural, 59

rights (cont.)
  substantive, 59
  voting, 77
Roman law, 9
rule of law, 51, 76
rule of recognition, 65–7
rules of law, 4–5

Scotland Act, 68
Scripture, 40–1
security, 49–55
self-correction, continuous, xiii, 9, 12, 16, 57, 61, 85
sovereignty, 6, 11–14, 18, 27–8, 63–7
  cession of state, 65
  legislative, 12, 26, 29
  Parliamentary, 3–4, 11–14, 18, 23–30
  and the European Union, 64–6
state power, 3–5, 83
  confinement, 16
  orderly development of, 9, 29, 57, 85
state security, *see* security.
state sovereignty, *see* sovereignty.
statute, xiii, 3–5, 11–17, 20–6, 29, 52, 55–7, 64–70, 73, 77–80
  constitutional, 68–9
  law, 3, 24–6, 46
Statute of Westminster, 65
statutory construction, *see* construction.
statutory powers, 23–5
Strasbourg, *see* European Court of Human Rights.
Straw, Jack, 72, 80
subservience, 73–5
Sumption, Lord, 24, 78–81
supremacy, 13, 29, 69
  of European law, 13, 69
  legislative, 14, 27–8, 67–8
Symmachus, Aurelius, xiv, 38–9, 56
syntax, 21–3

Terrorism Prevention and Investigation Measures, *see* TPIMs.
Thoburn case, 13, 66–71
threats, 4, 29, 31, 46–51, 54–8, 62–3, 71, 85
tolerance, 32–4, 45
TPIMs (Terrorism Prevention and Investigation Measures), 53–5
tranquillity of the State, 30–1, 51
tri-partite philosophy, 40
truth, xiv, 13, 25–7, 31, 38, 47–8, 56, 71

Ullah case, 74–6, 81–3
ultra vires doctrine, 16–17
unifying principle, xiv–5, 57
universal jurisprudence, 75
unquestioning commitment, 32–6, 39

Valentinian II, 56
validity, 4, 24, 65
  legal, 17
value(s), 21–2, 35, 42, 47–9, 63, 76, 82
voting rights, 77

Waldron, Jeremy, 27
Wednesbury review, 62
Wittgenstein, Ludwig, 40
writs, prerogative, 14–16

For EU product safety concerns, contact us at Calle de José Abascal, 56–1°, 28003 Madrid, Spain or eugpsr@cambridge.org.

www.ingramcontent.com/pod-product-compliance
Ingram Content Group UK Ltd.
Pitfield, Milton Keynes, MK11 3LW, UK
UKHW021856250926
475916UK00003B/11

* 9 7 8 1 1 0 7 0 7 7 7 2 0 *